趣味識字
Fun with Chinese
A Chinese Character Learning Curriculum

第六冊
Workbook 6

自序

我是一位在美國的自學媽媽,孩子的中文學習完全由我親自教導。

在傳統教學方式的薰陶下許多家長認為孩子學中文必須先從注音開始,往往也認為中文字筆畫眾多複雜對小孩來說太難。其實對幼兒來說每一個中文字都只是一個圖案,幼兒的記憶力非常強,認字對他們來說並不困難。

我自己的兩個孩子都是從認字開始學習中文的。當初我會設計趣味識字是因為在市面上並沒有找到令我完全滿意的教材,絕大多數的教材都是從注音符號或是筆畫簡單的字開始教學。雖然筆劃較少容易書寫但往往這些字在日常生活上並不常見,在孩子的世界裡更是沒有應用的機會。而市面上認字的教材卻普遍地缺乏動手的參與感。孩子在學習的過程中常常覺得教材枯燥乏味,既沒趣味又缺乏實用性。這樣的學習對孩子來說不但痛苦也沒有效率。使用這些教材後我發現自己一直在動手製作輔助教材來提昇孩子的學習興趣。

我一直深信一定要讓孩子覺得有趣和實用,他們才會有學習的動力,有了動力才會學得好。所以趣味識字的設計是以先教常用字的方式讓孩子能夠快速進入閱讀,因而發覺識字的實用性。當孩子懂得如何應用文字後,學習自信自然就提高了。製作輔助教材時為了幫助孩子加強對生字的記憶,除了使用字卡和遊戲的方式複習,我也設計了一系列的遊戲習題,而這些習題就是趣味識字誕生的前奏。

最後非常感謝您選擇趣味識字做為孩子的教材,也希望這套教材可以幫助您的孩子快樂學習中文。

Preface

I am a homeschooling mom in America who successfully taught my two children to read Chinese at a young age.

Many people think that learning Chinese must start with pinyin because Chinese characters are too complicated and believed to be too difficult for children. However, in children's minds, each Chinese character is just like a picture and memorization is not difficult for them.

Both my children learned to read Chinese beginning with character recognition, yet the process was not easy for me. Existing textbooks often start teaching with pinyin or start with rarely used characters with minimal strokes for writing. Books that emphasize character recognition also tend to be less interactive and less hands-on causing the learning process to be tedious and unmotivating for children. I found myself constantly needing to create my own teaching materials while using these textbooks; and this is the reason for the creation of Fun with Chinese.

Fun with Chinese is designed to teach the most commonly used Chinese characters first, quickly allowing children to be able to read meaningful phrases and sentences from the very beginning. Pictures and games are also used to help with character retention, and each lesson includes reading passages to review previously learned characters.

Today, I am sharing with you this wonderful system that I have used with my own children and hoping to make your child's Chinese learning an easy and enjoyable journey.

— Anchia Tai

關於英文翻譯

習題本中的句子都有中英雙語,希望讓中文不是很好的家長們也有辦法使用教材。其中朗讀句子練習中的英文翻譯也盡量讓句型和中文相對應幫助英文為母語的家長容易理解。

About the English Translations

The English translations in the workbooks are specifically designed in a way to closely match up with the Chinese sentence grammar structure. While this might make the translations grammatically incorrect in English, the design will help English speakers to learn and understand the Chinese sentences better.

關於筆順

本書中的國字筆順是依據中華民國教育部「常用國字標準字體筆順學習網」的筆劃順序彙編。中華民國教育部對於部分筆順有做調整,可能於傳統書寫筆順有所差異,不同華人地區的筆順也可能有所不同。如果本書中的筆順與家長所學的筆順有所差異,請自行調整教學。

About the Stroke Orders

The stroke orders of the characters in this workbook follow the stroke orders provided on the "Learning Program for Stroke Order of Frequently Used Chinese Characters" website of the Ministry of Education, R.O.C. (Taiwan). The authors are aware that there were changes to the stroke orders made by the Ministry of Education as well as regional differences in character stroke orders. Please feel free to make adjustments in teaching if the stroke orders are different in your region.

每當完成一課後請回到本頁將該課的愛心塗上顏色。
Please color a heart after you have completed a lesson.

叫 問 七 太 老 書 把 黃 狗 幾 文 本 車 八 所 弟 常 故 事 寫 經 已 黑 再 先

第一課

Lesson 1 Jiào – to call; to shout

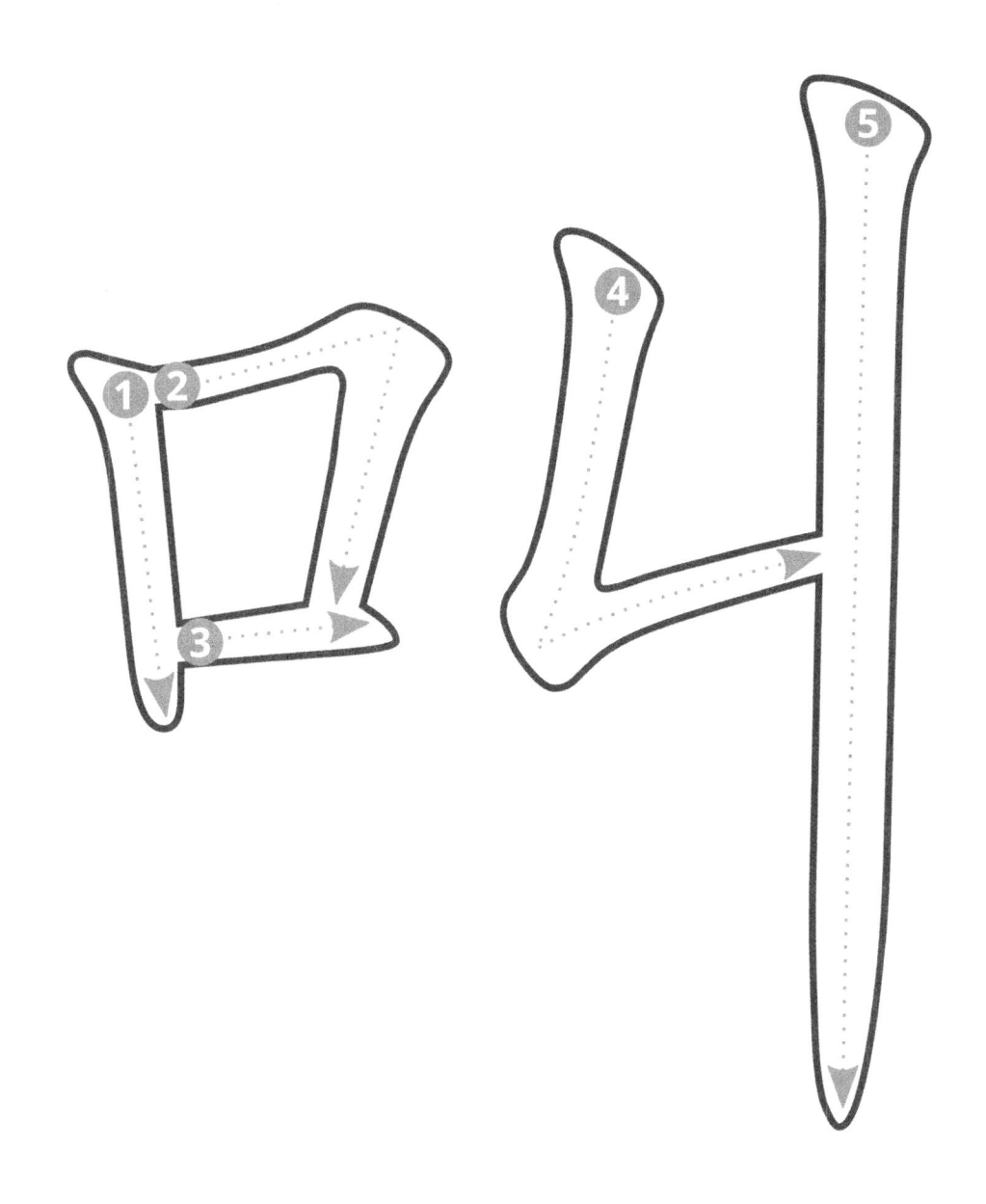

本書中的國字筆順是依據中華民國教育部「常用國字標準字體筆順學習網」的筆劃順序彙編。
The stroke orders of the characters in this workbook follow the stroke orders provided on the "Learning Program for Stroke Order of Frequently Used Chinese Characters" website of the Ministry of Education, R.O.C. (Taiwan).

跟著「叫」字從 ➡ 到 ★ 走出迷宮。
Follow the characters 叫 from the arrow to the star to exit the maze.

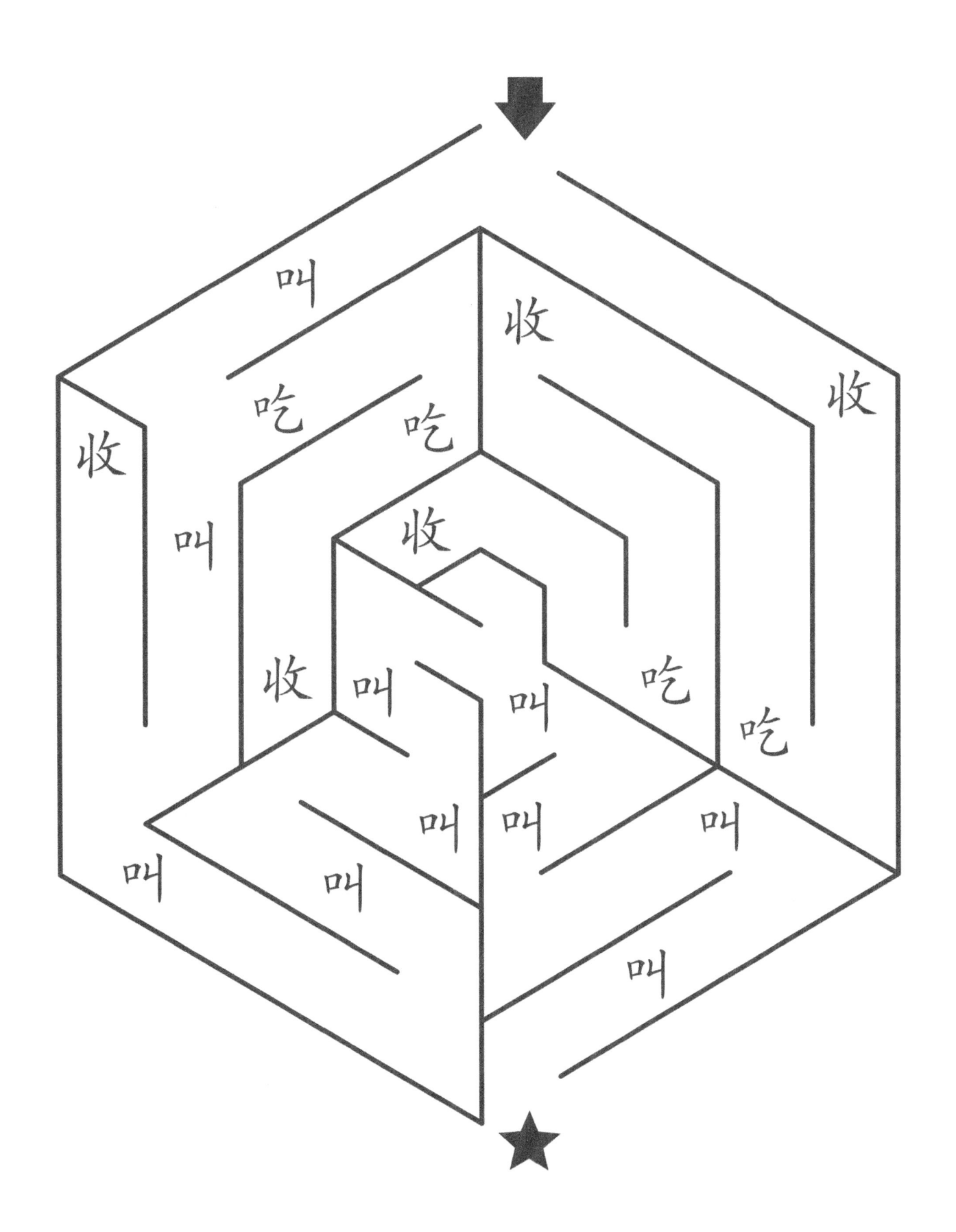

4

請連到正在叫的表情。
Find the path to the shouting face.

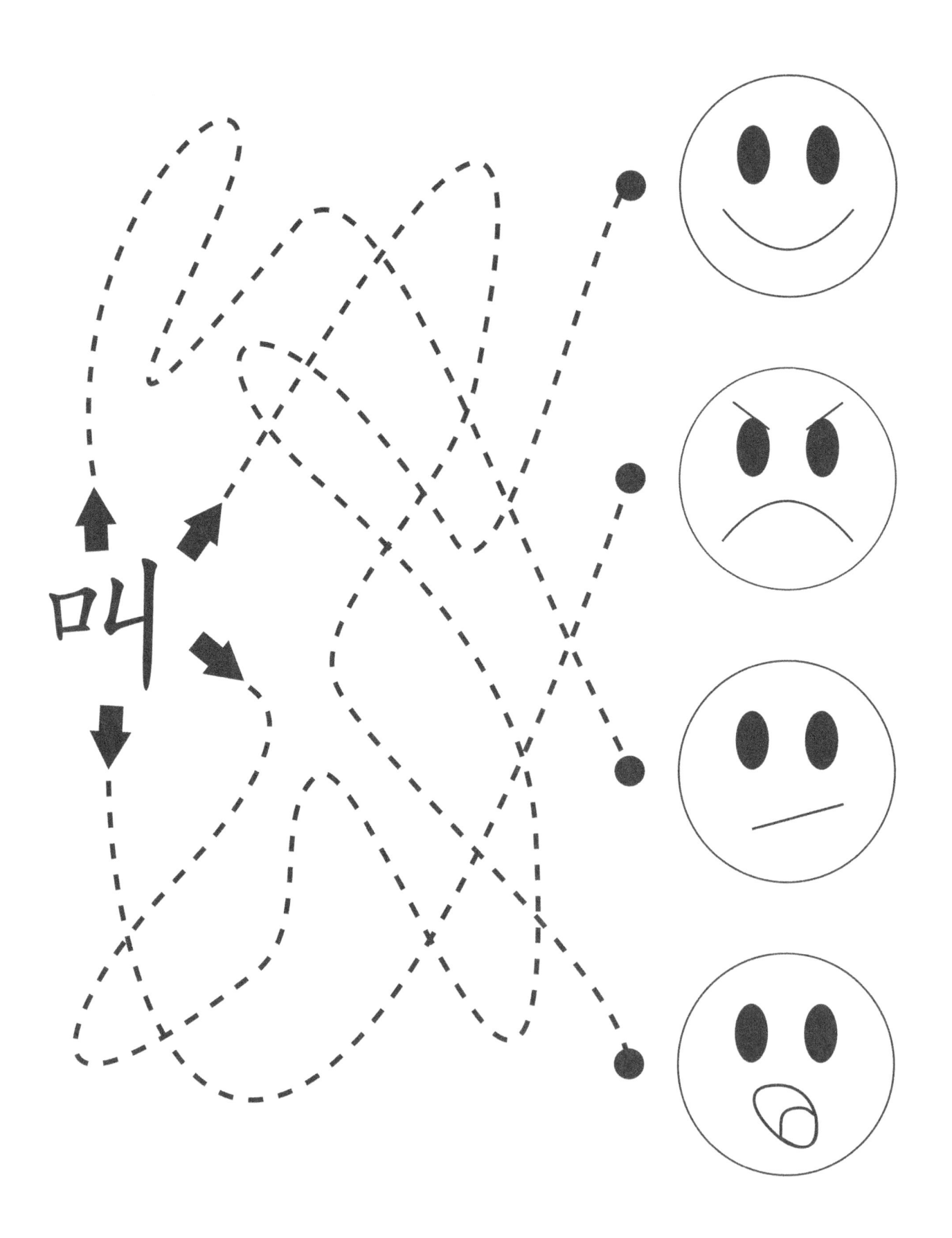

叫

唸唸看
Read-Aloud

- 媽媽叫我吃點心時不要說話。
Mom tells me not to talk while eating dessert.

- 也叫我不要用手吃。
(She) also tells me not to eat with my hands.

- 我說：「這樣是對的。」
I say, "This way is correct."

- 小白兔吃了六朵紅花。
The little white rabbit ate six red flowers.

- 兔子不會邊吃邊叫。
Rabbits don't eat and make sounds at same time.

恭喜你完成了這一課，請回到第一頁將本課的愛心塗上顏色。
Congratulations! You have completed a lesson. Please color the heart for this lesson on page 1.

第二課

Lesson 2 Wèn – to ask

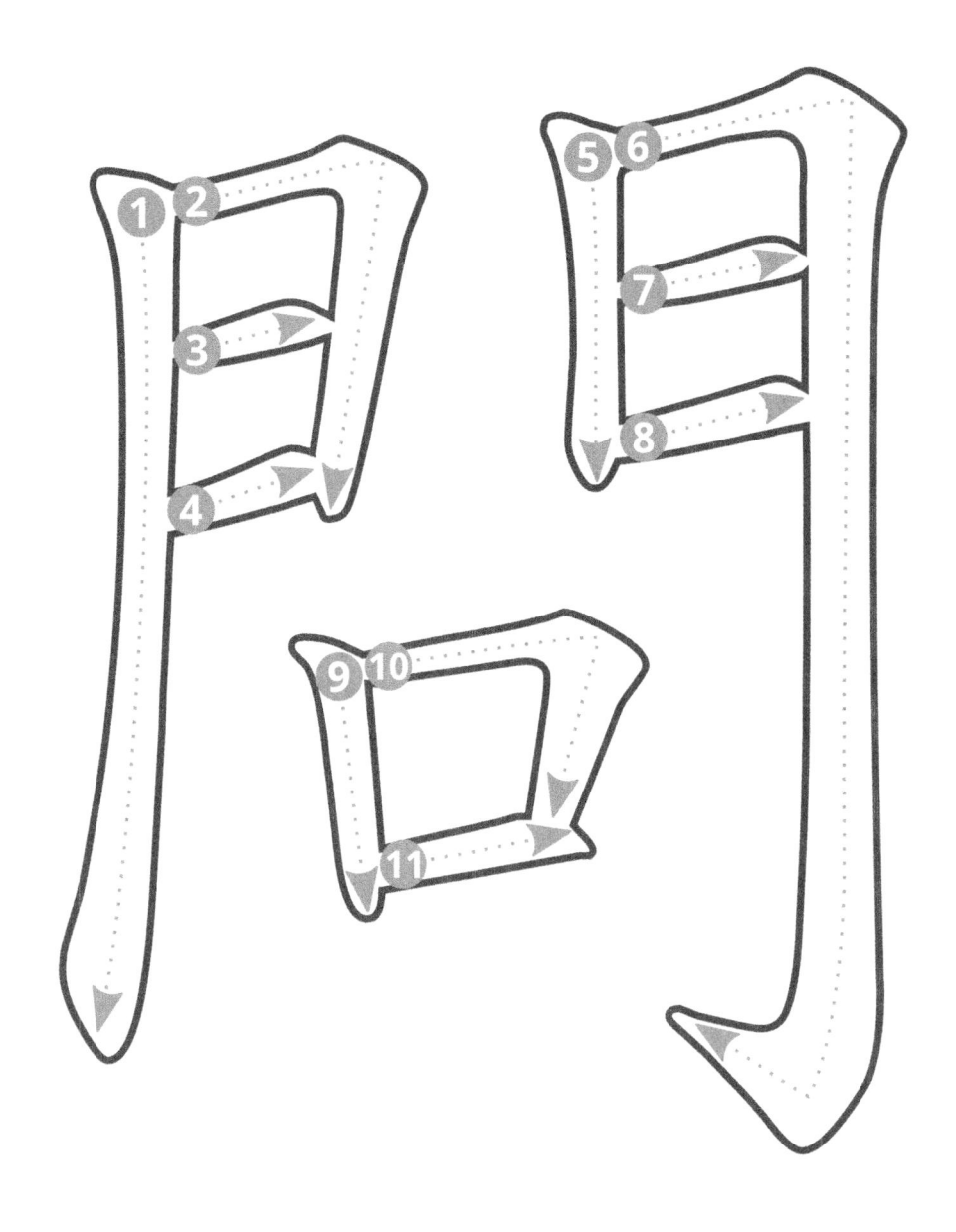

本書中的國字筆順是依據中華民國教育部「常用國字標準字體筆順學習網」的筆劃順序彙編。
The stroke orders of the characters in this workbook follow the stroke orders provided on the "Learning Program for Stroke Order of Frequently Used Chinese Characters" website of the Ministry of Education, R.O.C. (Taiwan).

將有「問」字的問號著色。
Color the question marks with the character 問.

找出「問」字圈出來。
Find the characters 問 and circle them.

口　門　　　黑

問　　問　　空
　　　　　　對
間　見　　　問
　　開　　　閒

唸唸看
Read-Aloud

- 爸爸問：「你的手裡有什麼？」
Dad asks, "What do you have in your hands?"

- 我說：「我的手裡有六隻愛叫的小鳥。」
I say, "I have six little birds that love to chirp in my hands."

- 爸爸又問：「小鳥的樣子可愛嗎？」
Dad asks again, "Do the little birds look cute?"

- 我說：「對，小鳥很可愛。」
I say, "Yes, the little birds are very cute."

- 小鳥飛回樹上的家了。
The little birds flew back to their home on the tree.

恭喜你完成了這一課，請回到第一頁將本課的愛心塗上顏色。
Congratulations! You have completed a lesson. Please color the heart for this lesson on page 1.

第三課

Lesson 3 Qī – seven

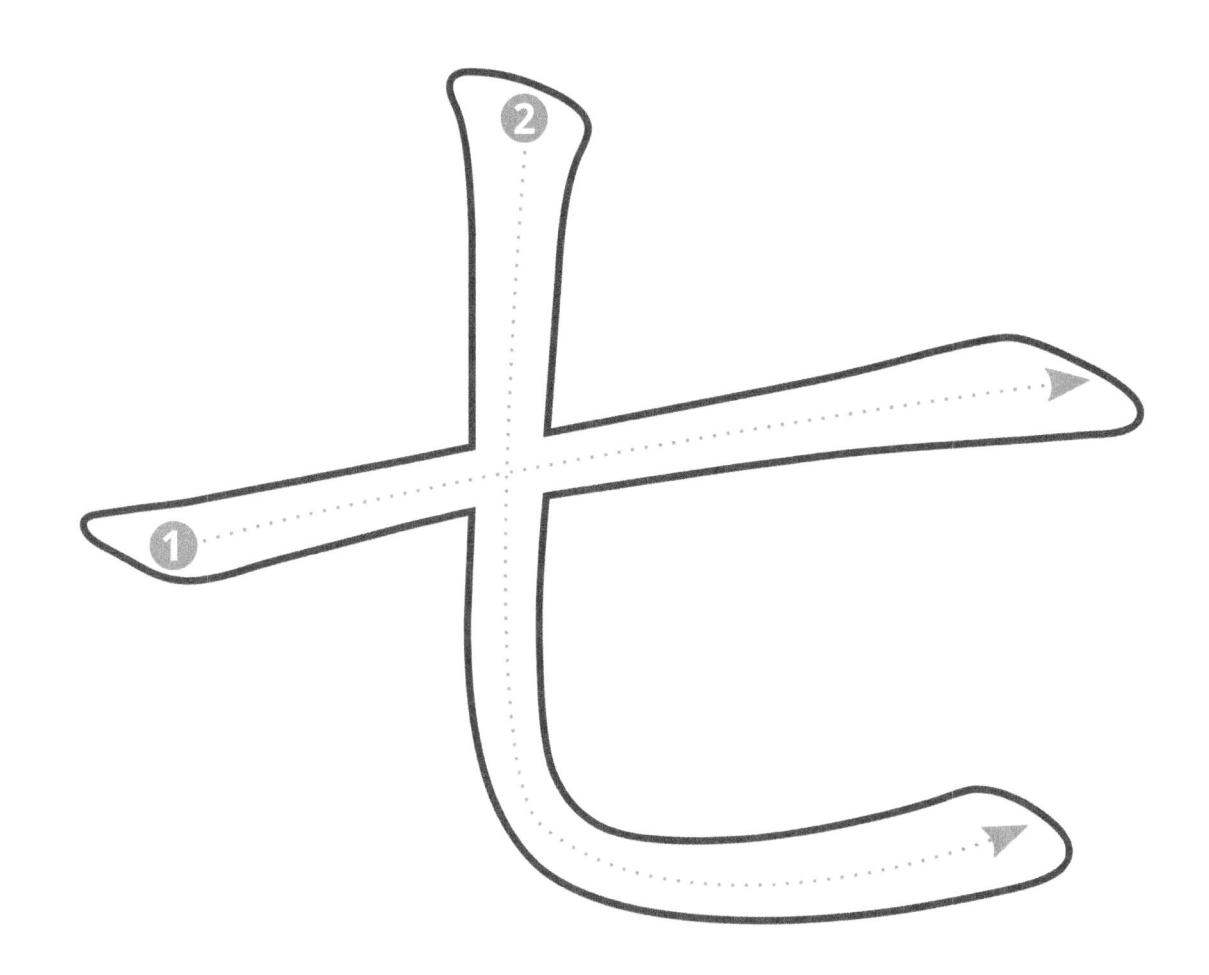

本書中的國字筆順是依據中華民國教育部「常用國字標準字體筆順學習網」的筆劃順序彙編。
The stroke orders of the characters in this workbook follow the stroke orders provided on the "Learning Program for Stroke Order of Frequently Used Chinese Characters" website of the Ministry of Education, R.O.C. (Taiwan).

請圈出正確的數量。
Please circle the correct quantities.

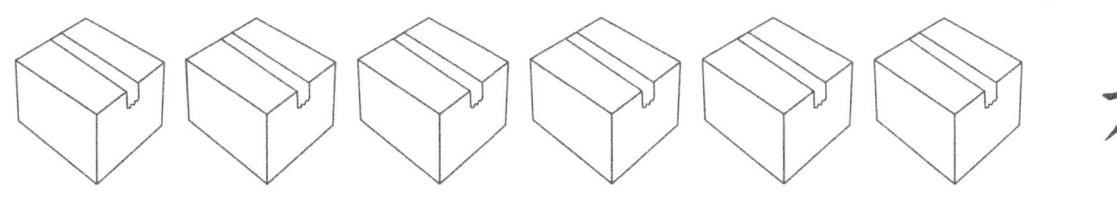

♪♪♪♪♪♪♪　　七／五

🧸🧸🧸🧸🧸🧸　　七／六

⚽⚽⚽⚽⚽　　三／五

BOOK BOOK BOOK　　三／四

📦📦📦📦📦📦　　六／七

12

連連看
Please connect the dots to complete the picture.

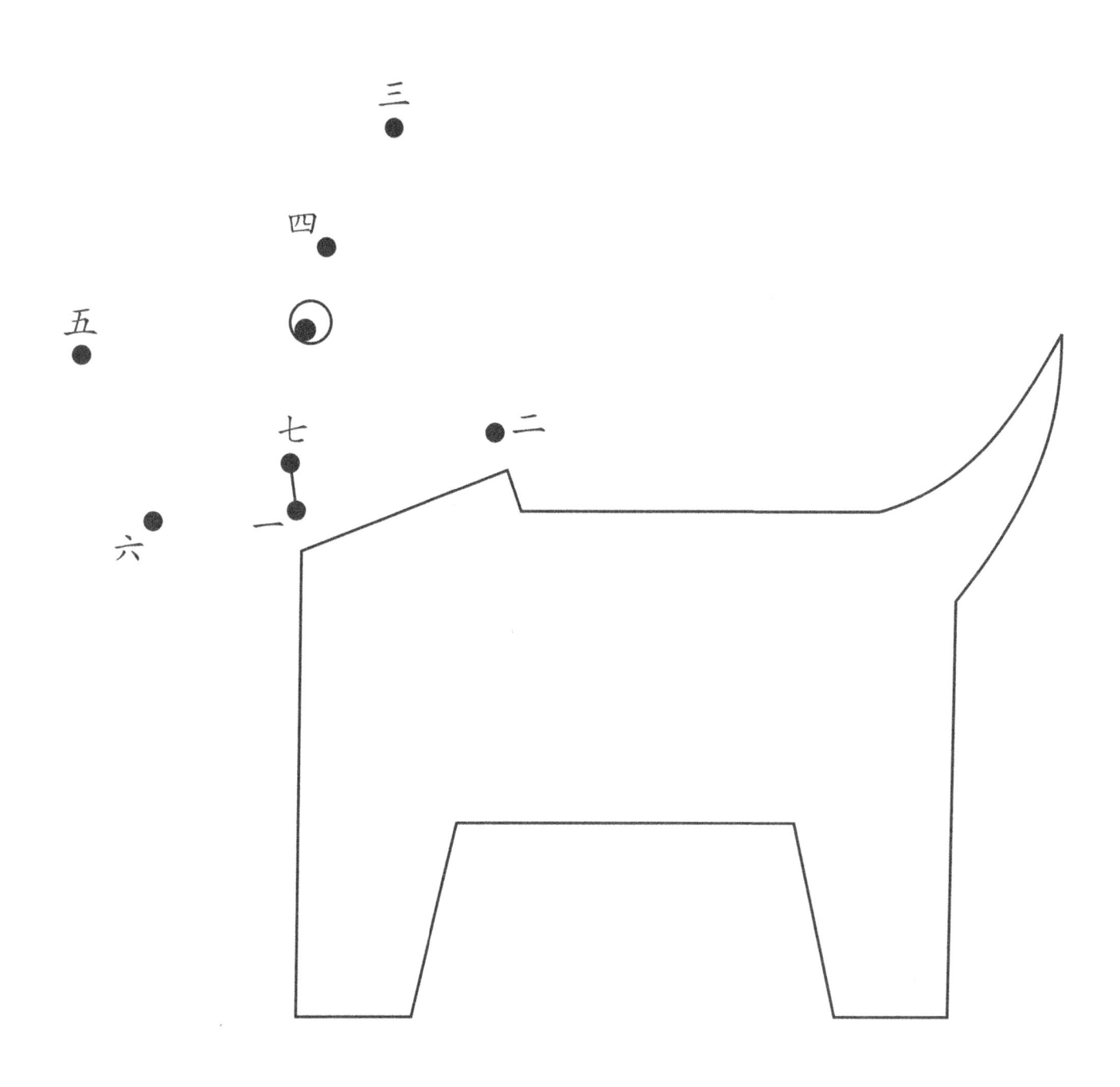

唸唸看
Read-Aloud

- 他問：「貓有七隻手嗎？」
  He asks, "Do cats have seven hands?"

- 我說：「不對，貓沒有七隻手。」
  I say, "No, cats do not have seven hands."

- 他又問：「兔子會和貓一樣叫嗎？」
  He asks again, "Do rabbits meow like cats do?"

- 我說：「兔子不會叫。」
  I say, "Rabbits do not meow."

- 兔子只能跑和跳。
  Rabbits can only run and hop.

恭喜你完成了這一課，請回到第一頁將本課的愛心塗上顏色。
Congratulations! You have completed a lesson. Please color the heart for this lesson on page 1.

第四課

Lesson 4 Tài – too; overly

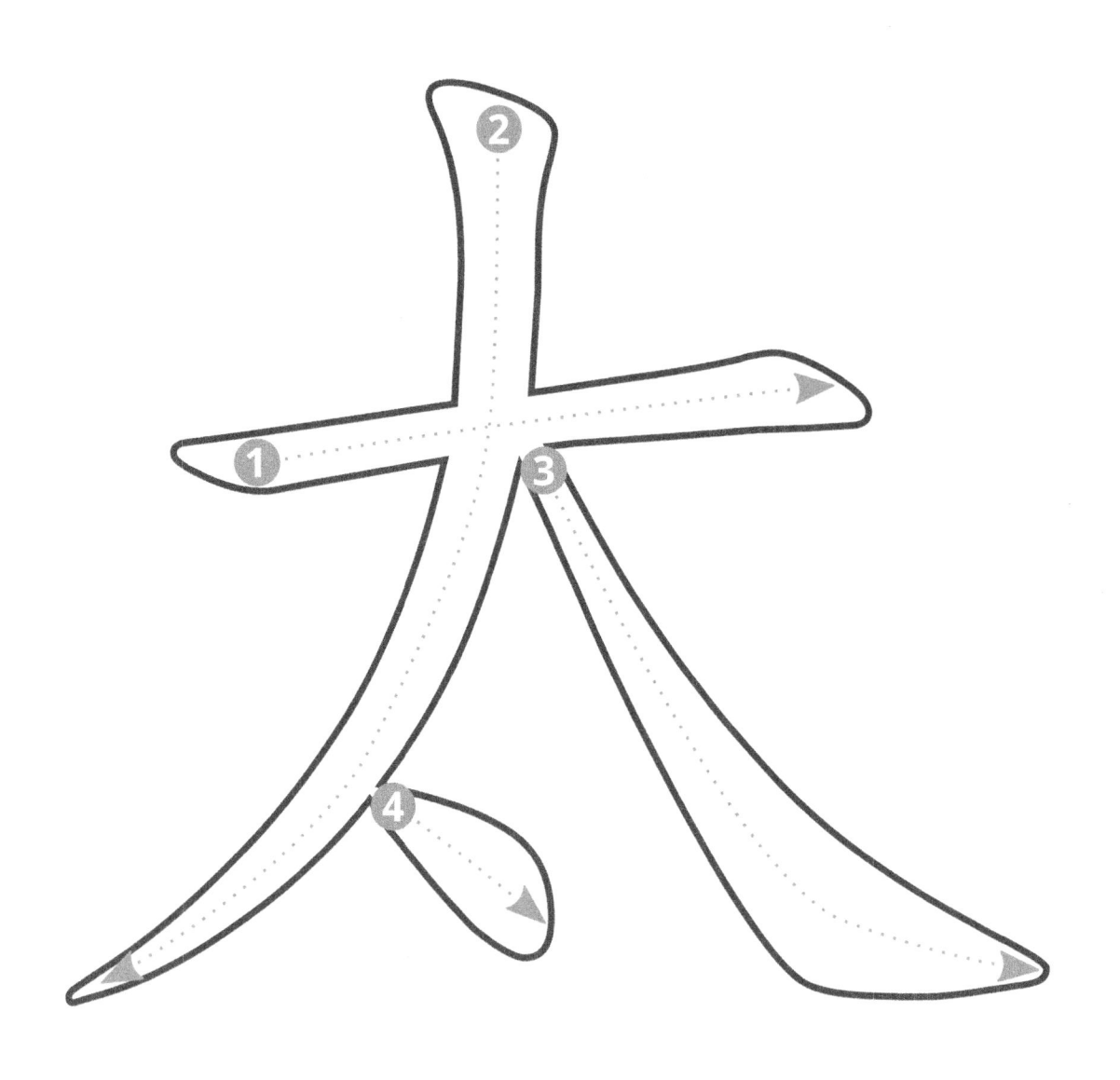

本書中的國字筆順是依據中華民國教育部「常用國字標準字體筆順學習網」的筆劃順序彙編。
The stroke orders of the characters in this workbook follow the stroke orders provided on the "Learning Program for Stroke Order of Frequently Used Chinese Characters" website of the Ministry of Education, R.O.C. (Taiwan).

請將有「太」字的地方著色。
Color the areas with the character 太.

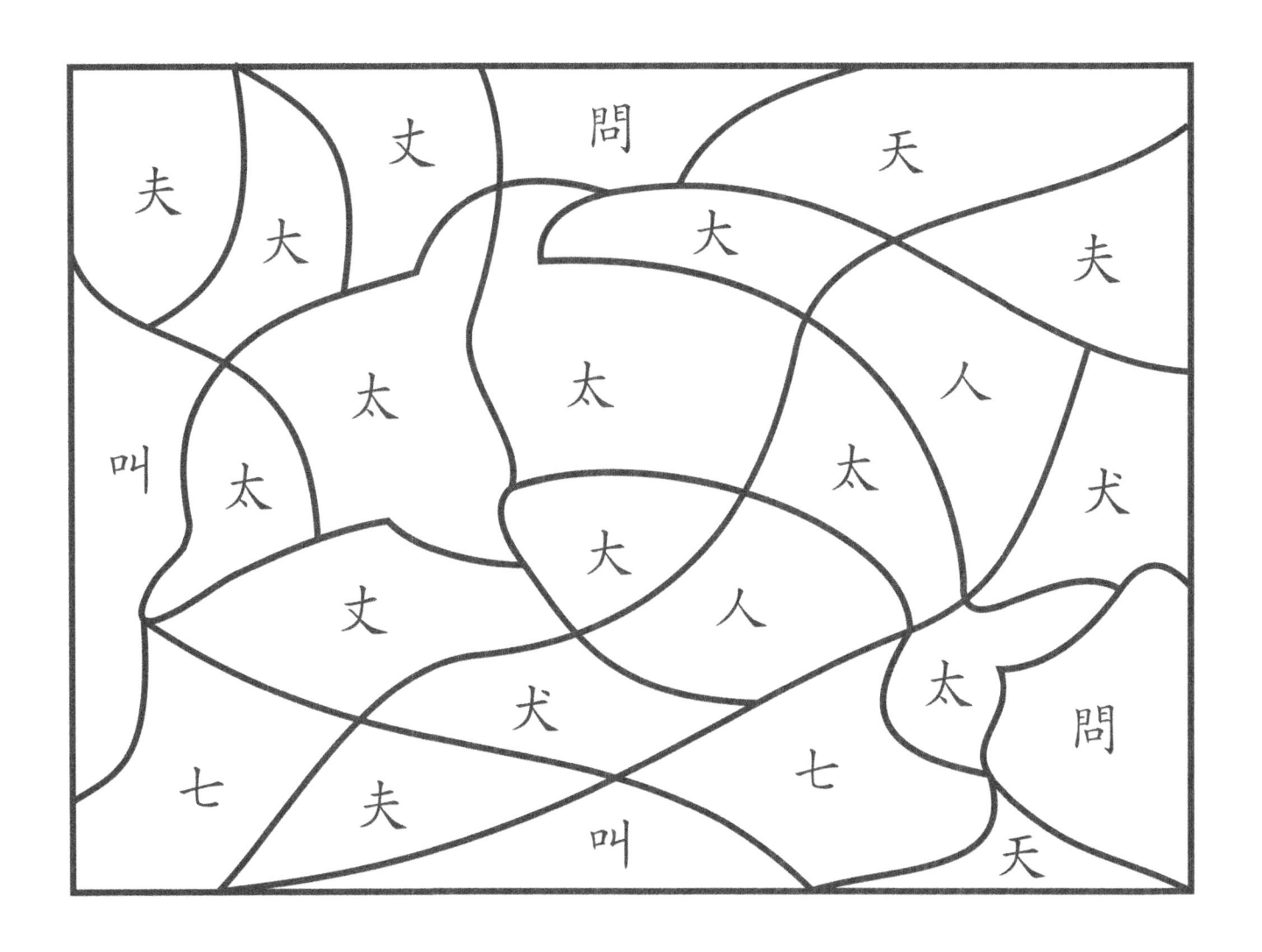

16

請將下方的字格剪下來，分別貼到對應的位置。
Cut out the phrases at the bottom and paste them to the correct pictures.

| 太多 | 太大 | 太高 | 太長 | 太小 |

唸唸看
Read-Aloud

- 那隻藍色的鳥吃得太多了。
That blue bird ate too much.

- 我問：「他會不會飛不動？」
I ask, "Will it not be able to fly?"

- 小鳥跳到山對面去了。
The little bird hopped to the other side of the mountain.

- 他跳的樣子看起來好可愛。
He looked very cute when he hopped.

- 以後叫他不要吃太多了。
From now on, tell it not to eat so much.

恭喜你完成了這一課，請回到第一頁將本課的愛心塗上顏色。
Congratulations! You have completed a lesson. Please color the heart for this lesson on page 1.

第五課

Lesson 5 Lǎo – old; aged; always

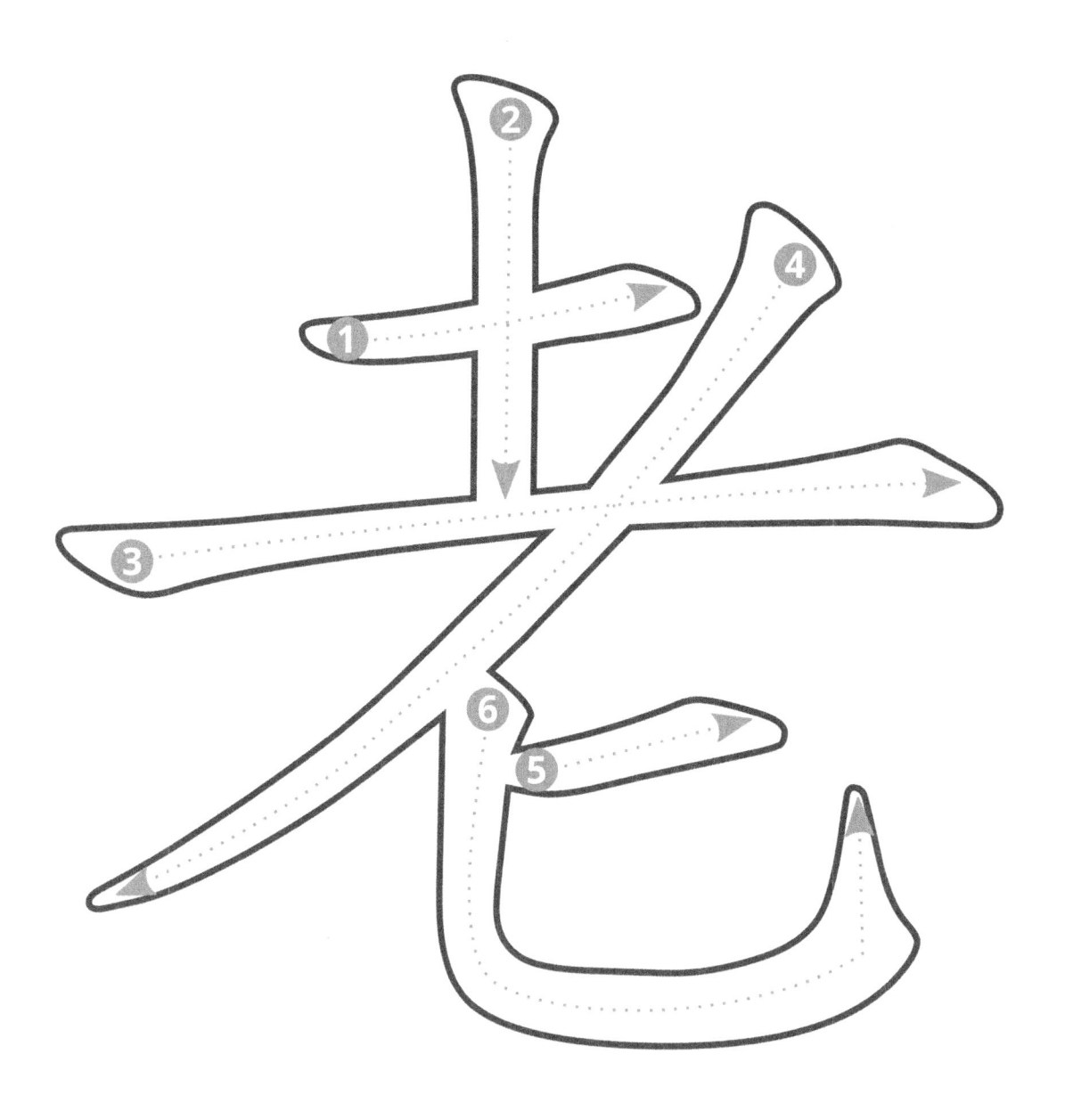

本書中的國字筆順是依據中華民國教育部「常用國字標準字體筆順學習網」的筆劃順序彙編。
The stroke orders of the characters in this workbook follow the stroke orders provided on the "Learning Program for Stroke Order of Frequently Used Chinese Characters" website of the Ministry of Education, R.O.C. (Taiwan).

19

連連看
Connect the characters to the correct pictures.

老

小

20

請圈出與文字相對應的圖案。
Circle the pictures that match the phrase.

老人家

請圈出與文字相對應的圖案。
Circle the pictures that match the phrase.

唸唸看
Read-Aloud

- 有一個老太太問我叫什麼。
  An old lady asked for my name.

- 我說我叫小明。
  I said my name is Ming.

- 老太太說我的樣子很可愛。
  The old lady said I look very cute.

- 我是一個好學生。
  I am a good student.

- 我七點就上學去了。
  I go to school at seven o'clock.

恭喜你完成了這一課，請回到第一頁將本課的愛心塗上顏色。
Congratulations! You have completed a lesson. Please color the heart for this lesson on page 1.

第六課

Lesson 6 Jǐ – how many; how much; some
Jī – almost

本書中的國字筆順是依據中華民國教育部「常用國字標準字體筆順學習網」的筆劃順序彙編。
The stroke orders cpf the characters in this workbook follow the stroke orders provided on the "Learning Program for Stroke Order of Frequently Used Chinese Characters" website of the Ministry of Education, R.O.C. (Taiwan).

請將下方的字格剪下來讓孩子選擇正確的字貼上。
Please cut out the characters at the bottom and paste the correct ones.

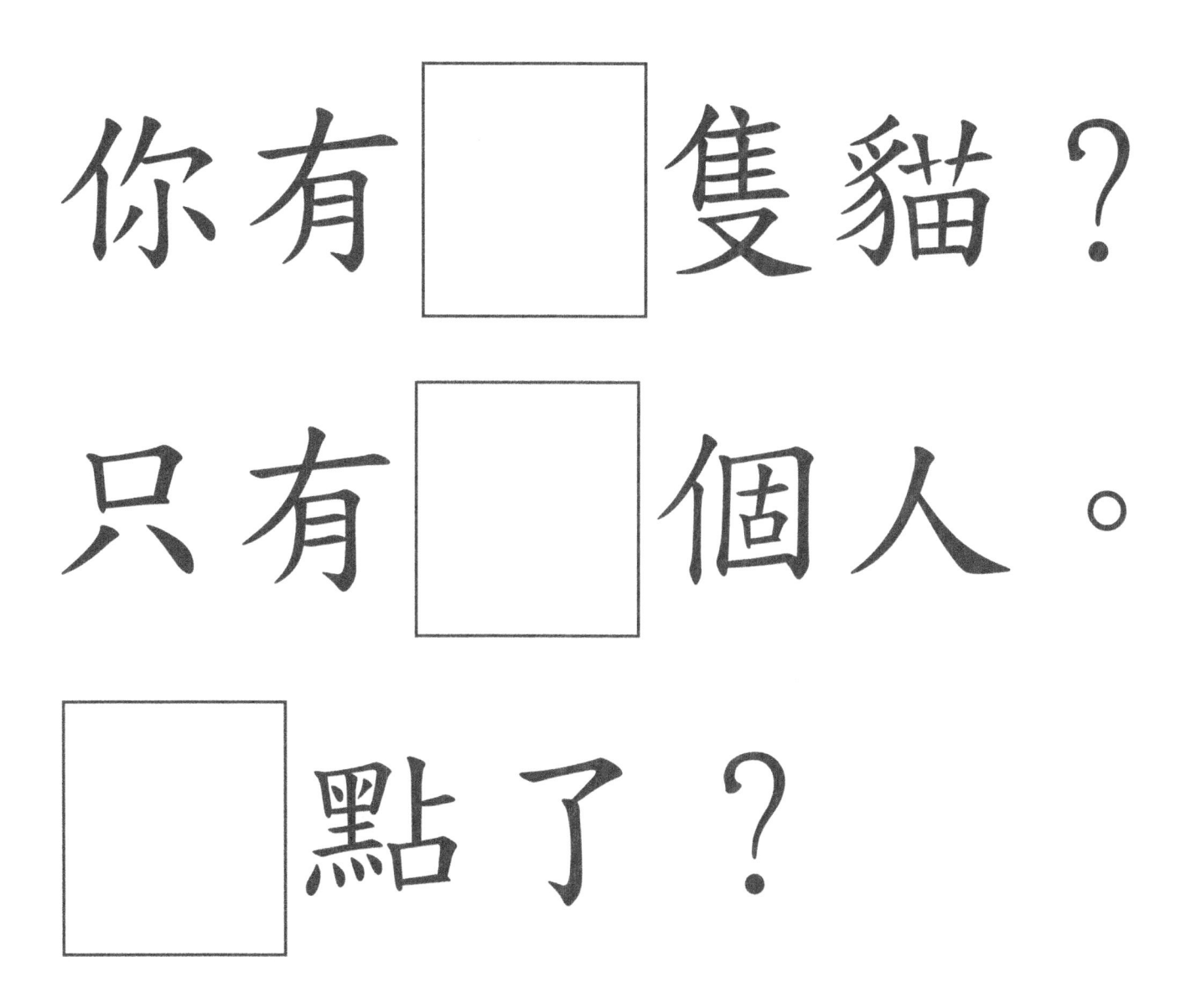

你有☐隻貓？

只有☐個人。

☐點了？

| 幾 | 機 | 幾 | 機 | 幾 |

24

將「幾」字塗色，幫毛蟲找到香菇。
Color the characters 幾 to find the path to the mushroom.

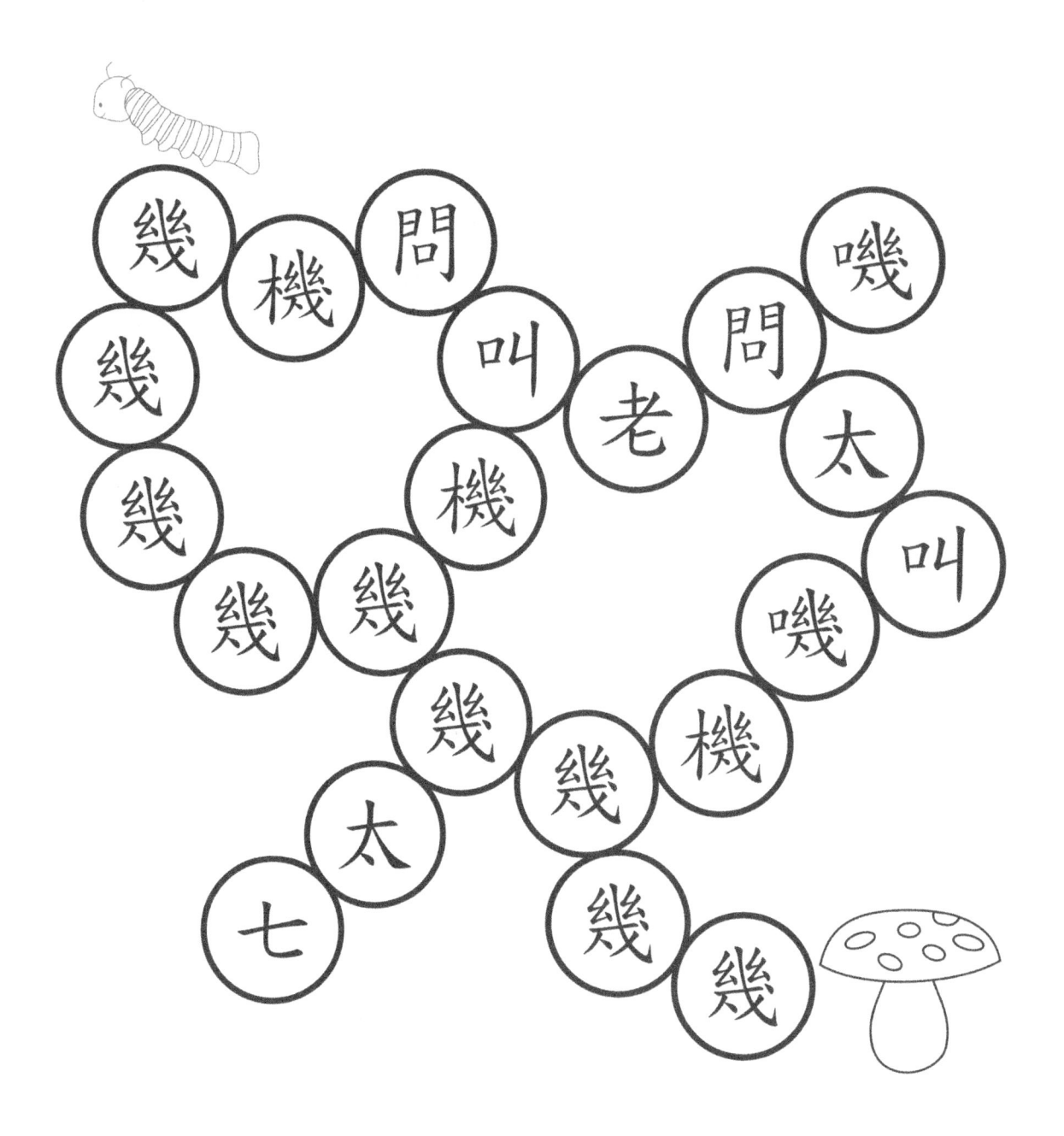

唸唸看
Read-Aloud

- 我問：「還有幾天我會過生日？」

  I ask, "How many more days are there until my birthday?"

- 媽媽老是對我說：「七天以後。」

  Mom keeps on saying to me, "Seven days later."

- 生日會時我想叫爸爸唱歌。

  During my birthday party, I want to ask Dad to sing.

- 爸爸的樣子太開心了。

  Dad looks very happy.

- 有幾個人會來我的生日會？

  How many people will come to my birthday party?

恭喜你完成了這一課，請回到第一頁將本課的愛心塗上顏色。
Congratulations! You have completed a lesson. Please color the heart for this lesson on page 1.

第七課

Lesson 7 Gǒu – dog

本書中的國字筆順是依據中華民國教育部「常用國字標準字體筆順學習網」的筆劃順序彙編。
The stroke orders of the characters in this workbook follow the stroke orders provided on the "Learning Program for Stroke Order of Frequently Used Chinese Characters" website of the Ministry of Education, R.O.C. (Taiwan).

請圈出與圖案對應的文字。
Please circle the characters that best describe the pictures.

狗 / 貓

狗 / 貓

狗 / 貓

狗 / 貓

狗 / 貓

狗 / 貓

28

找出到達「狗」字的路。
Find the path leading to the character 狗.

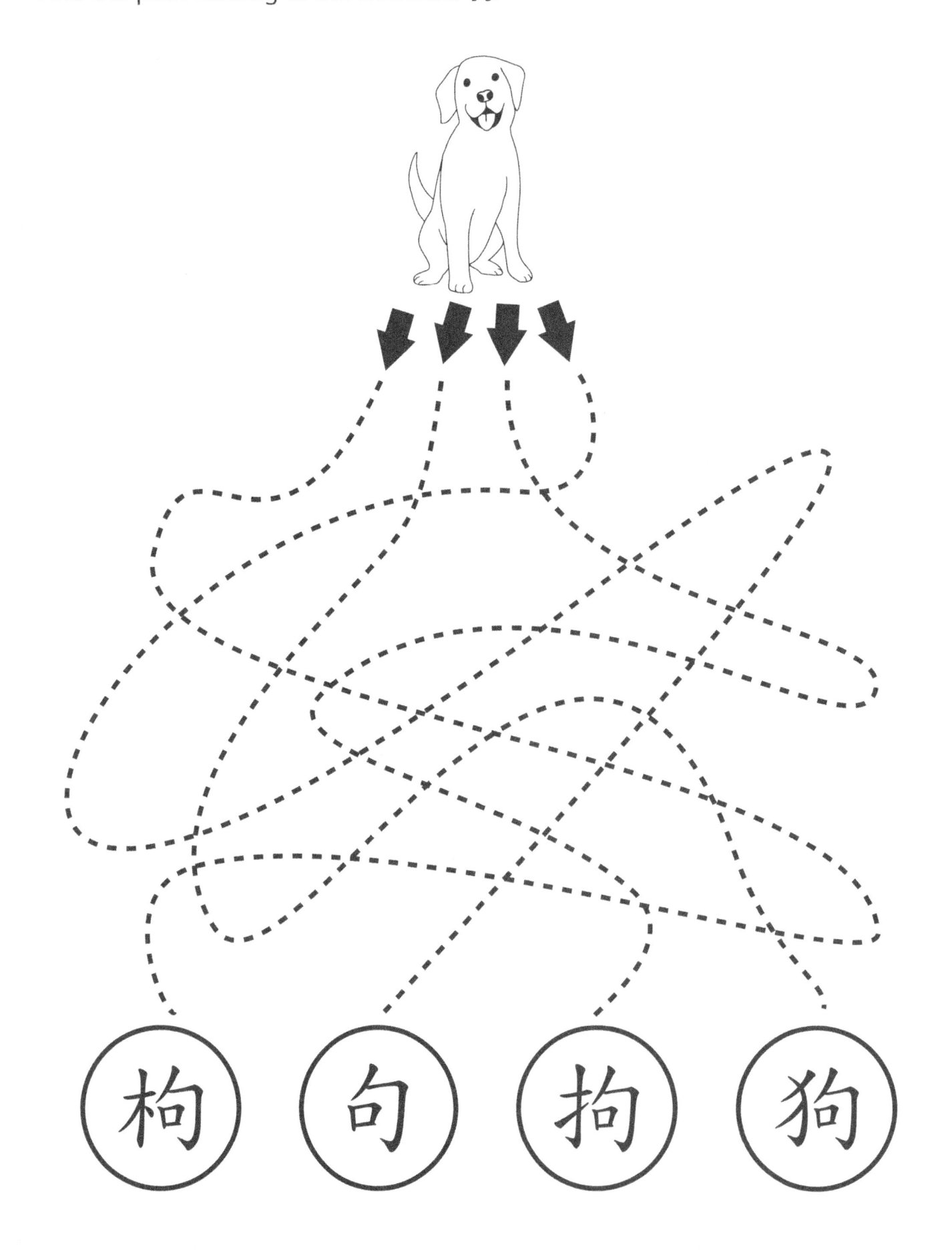

| 枸 | 句 | 拘 | 狗 |

唸唸看
Read-Aloud

- 我問：「你家有幾隻小狗？」
  I ask, "How many little dogs do you have in your home?"

- 你說：「我家有七隻小狗。」
  You say, "I have seven little dogs in my home."

- 有一隻小狗老是愛叫。
  One of the little dogs loves to bark all the time.

- 我對他說：「不要叫了。」
  I say to it, "Do not bark."

- 爸爸說：「太好了。」
  Dad says, "Great."

恭喜你完成了這一課，請回到第一頁將本課的愛心塗上顏色。
Congratulations! You have completed a lesson. Please color the heart for this lesson on page 1.

第八課

Lesson 8 Huáng – yellow

本書中的國字筆順是依據中華民國教育部「常用國字標準字體筆順學習網」的筆劃順序彙編。
The stroke orders of the characters in this workbook follow the stroke orders provided on the "Learning Program for Stroke Order of Frequently Used Chinese Characters" website of the Ministry of Education, R.O.C. (Taiwan).

請將香蕉塗上黃色並唸出下方的文字。
Please color the banana yellow then read aloud the characters at the bottom.

我是黃色的

32

請將三個相同的字連成一線。
Please connect the same characters to win the tic-tac-toe.

紅	藍	藍
黃	黃	黃
紅	藍	紅

唸唸看
Read-Aloud

- 小黃狗老是愛在路邊叫。
  The little yellow dog loves to bark on the side of the road all the time.

- 他叫了好幾天。
  It barked for several days.

- 小黃狗叫著叫著就走開了。
  The little yellow dog barked and barked and then walked away.

- 我們都說:「太好了。」
  We all say, "Great."

- 你不用生氣了。
  You don't need to be angry.

恭喜你完成了這一課,請回到第一頁將本課的愛心塗上顏色。
Congratulations! You have completed a lesson. Please color the heart for this lesson on page 1.

第九課

Lesson 9 Bǎ – to hold; handle; particle marking the following noun as a direct object

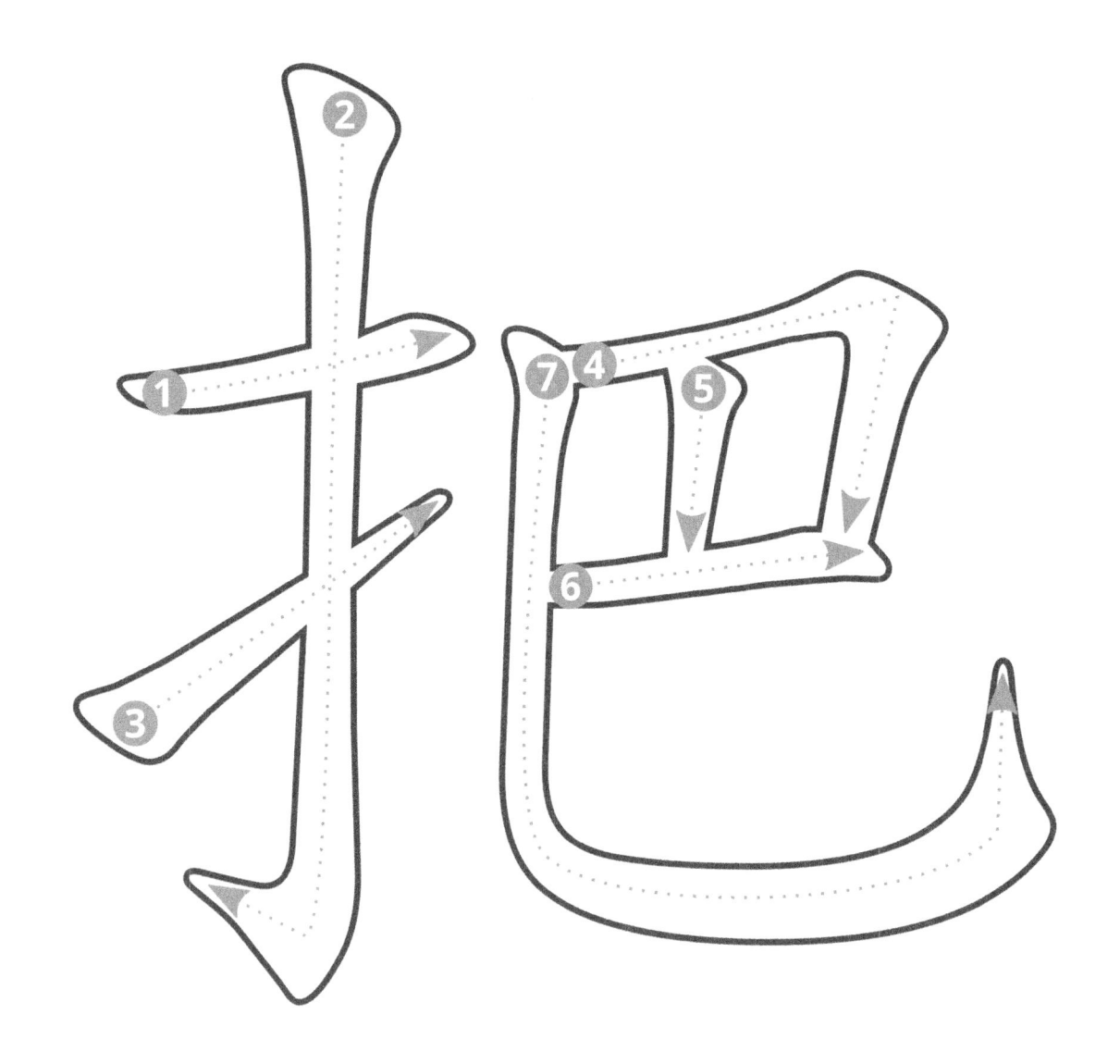

本書中的國字筆順是依據中華民國教育部「常用國字標準字體筆順學習網」的筆劃順序彙編。
The stroke orders of the characters in this workbook follow the stroke orders provided on the "Learning Program for Stroke Order of Frequently Used Chinese Characters" website of the Ministry of Education, R.O.C. (Taiwan).

請圈出有把手的東西並唸出下方的文字。
Please circle the objects with handles and read aloud the characters below.

把手

36

將「把」字塗色，幫海豹找到魚。
Color the characters 把 to find the path to the fish.

叫	把	把		七	
	把			樣	
太	把	把	把	老	幾
老			把		歌
點	狗	把	把	問	
		把			
兒	老	把	把		

唸唸看
Read-Aloud

- 草地上有兩隻老黃狗。
  There are two old yellow dogs on the grass field.

- 他們從幾天前就在那裡了。
  They have been there since several days ago.

- 他們都沒有走開。
  They both have not left.

- 還把我的點心給吃了。
  (They) even ate my dessert.

- 我對他們說:「把我的點心還給我。」
  I say to them, "Give me back my dessert."

恭喜你完成了這一課,請回到第一頁將本課的愛心塗上顏色。
Congratulations! You have completed a lesson. Please color the heart for this lesson on page 1.

第十課

Lesson 10 Shū – book

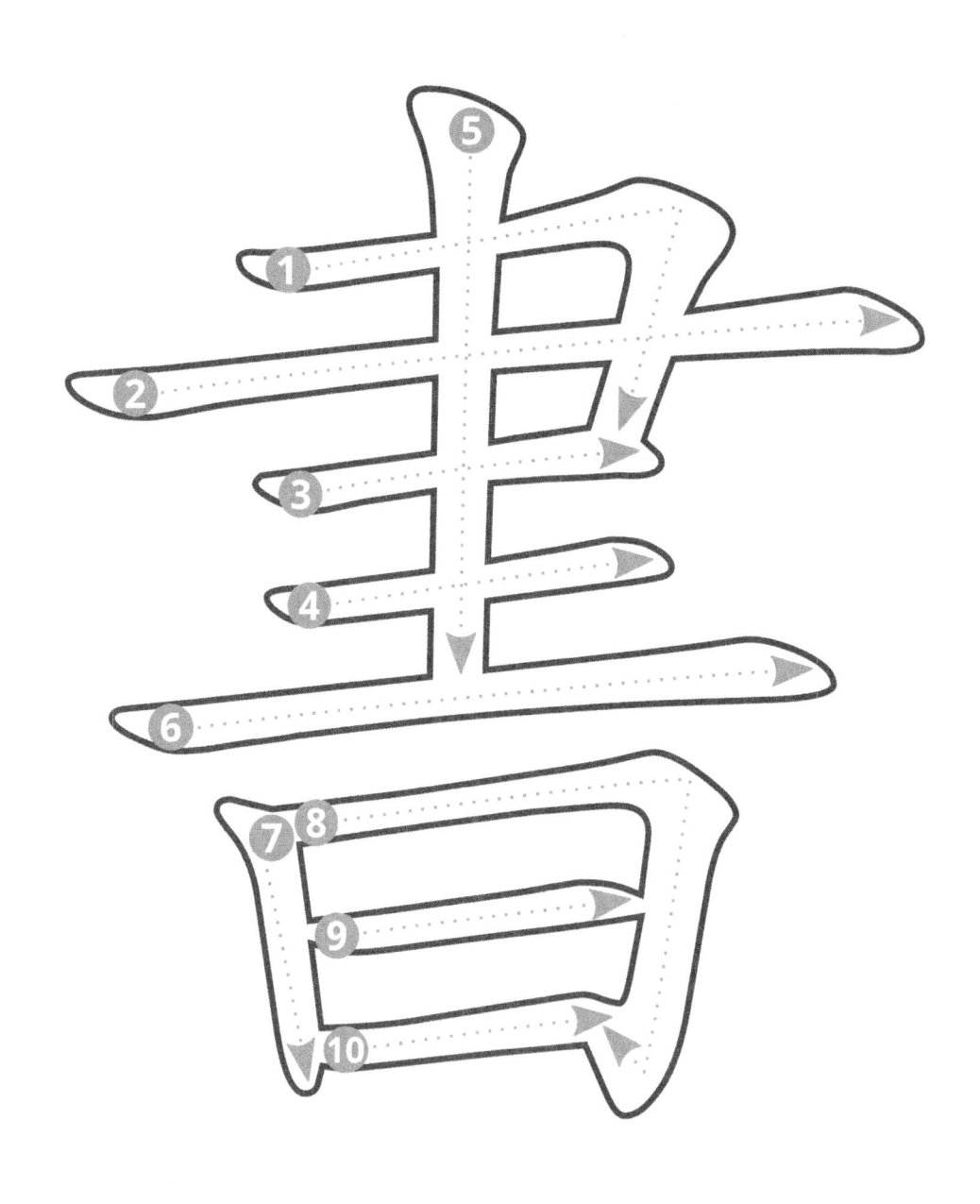

本書中的國字筆順是依據中華民國教育部「常用國字標準字體筆順學習網」的筆劃順序彙編。
The stroke orders of the characters in this workbook follow the stroke orders provided on the "Learning Program for Stroke Order of Frequently Used Chinese Characters" website of the Ministry of Education, R.O.C. (Taiwan).

跟著「書」字從 ➡ 到 ★ 走出迷宮。
Follow the characters 書 from the arrow to the star to exit the maze.

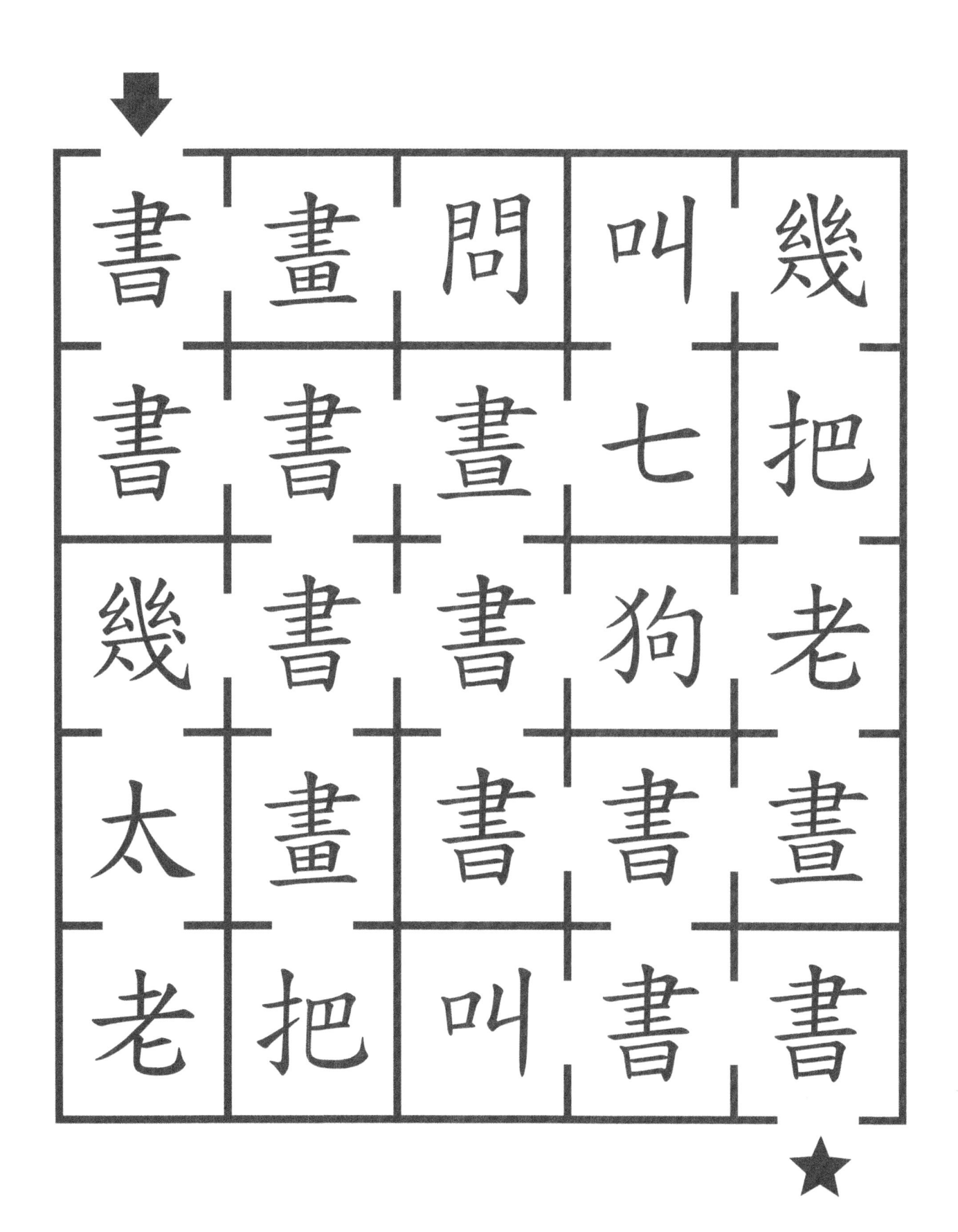

書	畫	問	叫	幾
書	書	畫	七	把
幾	書	書	狗	老
太	畫	書	書	畫
老	把	叫	書	書

40

連連看一樣的字。
Draw a line to the matching character.

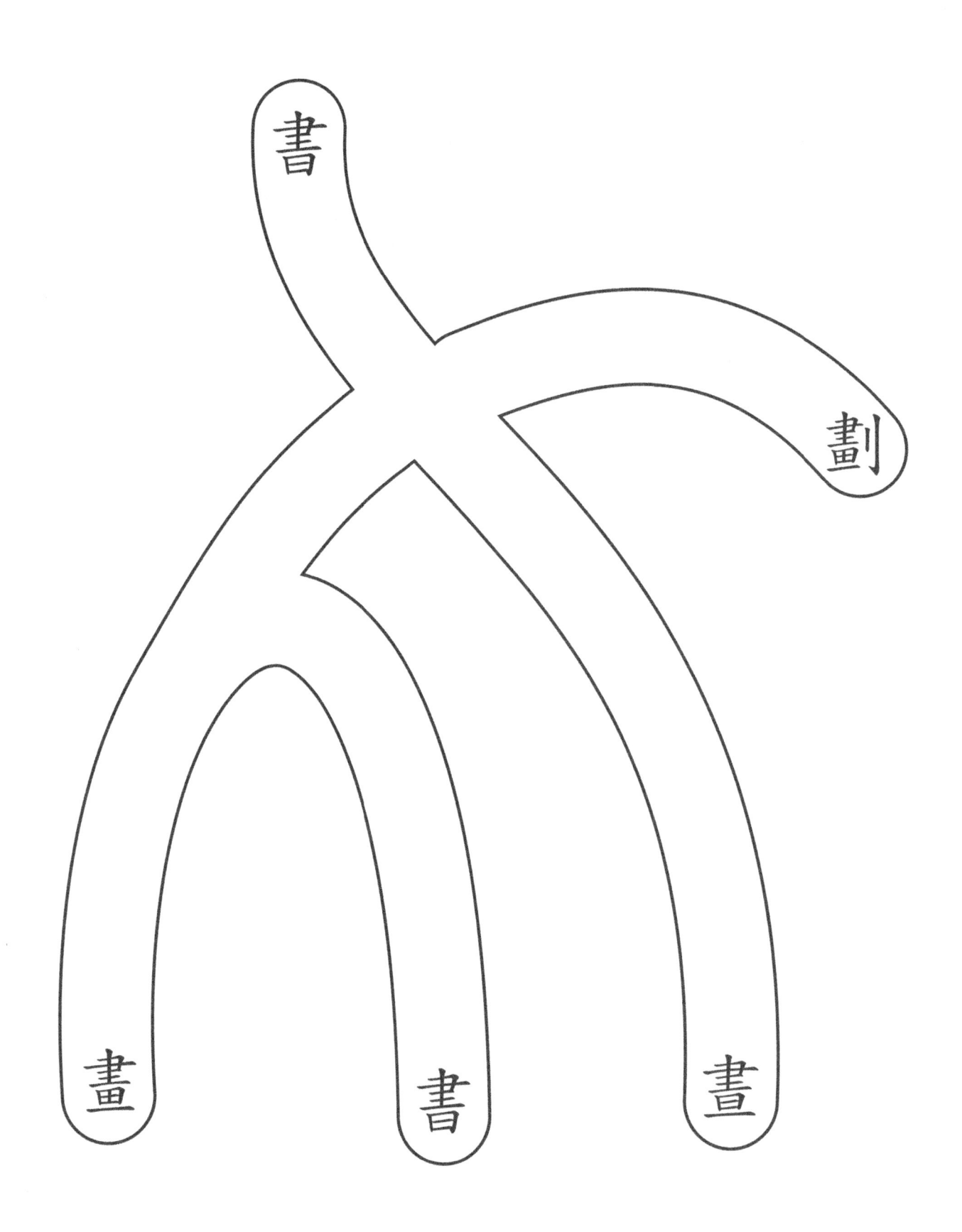

書　　　　　　　劃

畫　　　書　　　畫

唸唸看
Read-Aloud

- 幾天前，狗兒把我的書吃了。
  A few days ago, the little dog ate my book.

- 他吃的是我愛看的書。
  The book it ate is a book I love to read.

- 吃了以後他就跑出去了。
  It ran out after eating (my book).

- 也把外面的黃花給吃了。
  (It) also ate the yellow flowers outside.

- 媽媽聽到了真的好生氣。
  Mom got really angry after she heard it.

恭喜你完成了這一課，請回到第一頁將本課的愛心塗上顏色。
Congratulations! You have completed a lesson. Please color the heart for this lesson on page 1.

第十一課

Lesson 11 Wén – culture; language; writing; literary

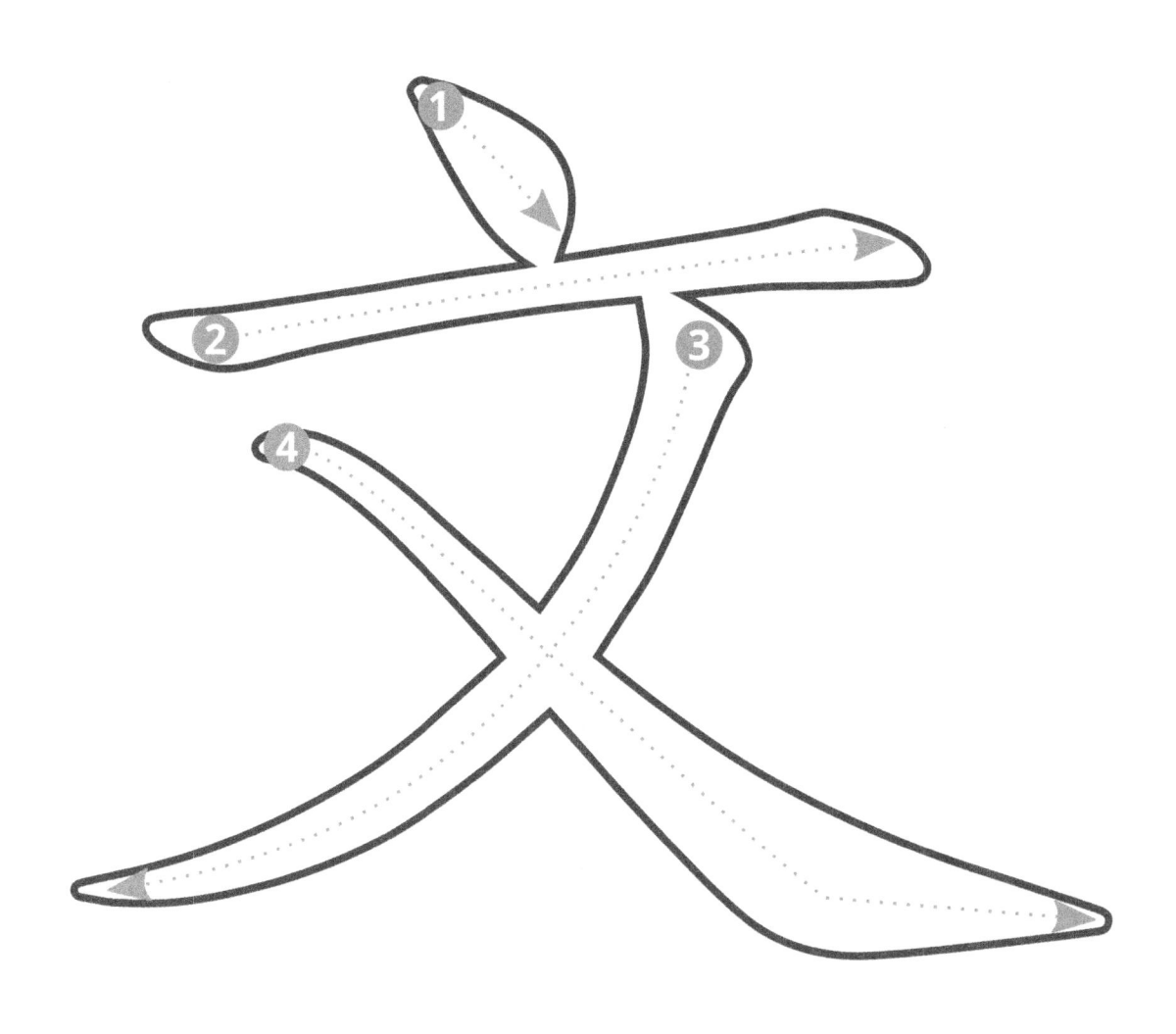

本書中的國字筆順是依據中華民國教育部「常用國字標準字體筆順學習網」的筆劃順序彙編。
The stroke orders of the characters in this workbook follow the stroke orders provided on the "Learning Program for Stroke Order of Frequently Used Chinese Characters" website of the Ministry of Education, R.O.C. (Taiwan).

跟著「文」字從 ➡ 到 ★ 走出迷宮。
Follow the characters 文 from the arrow to the star to exit the maze.

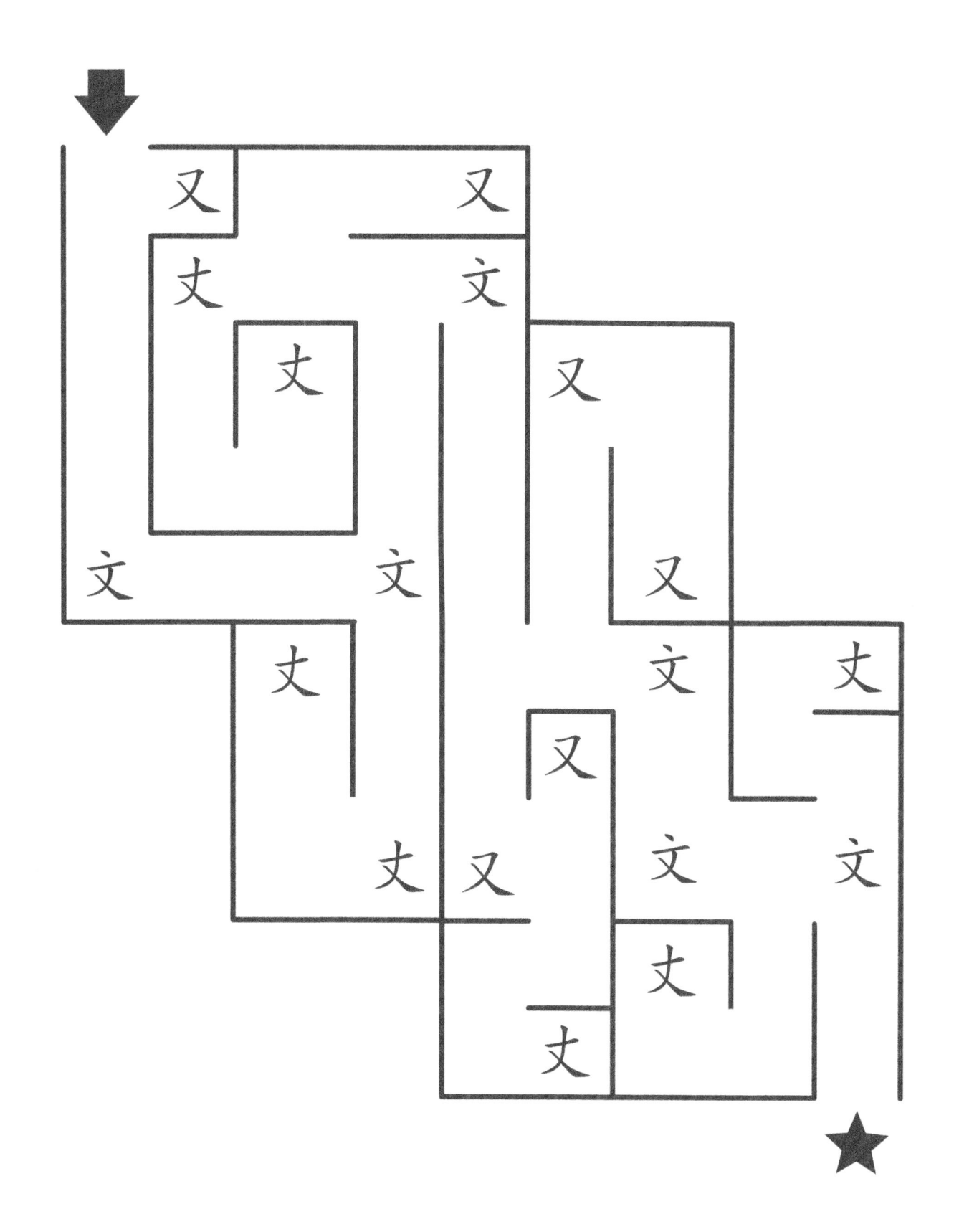

44

連連看一樣的字。
Draw lines to connect the matching characters.

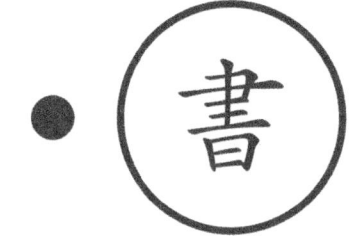

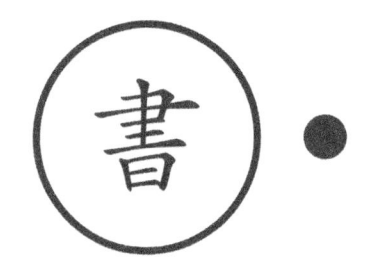

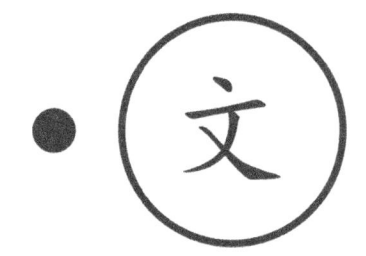

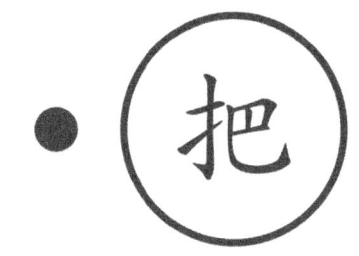

文　　　　　　　　　　書

書　　　　　　　　　　文

把　　　　　　　　　　把

唸唸看
Read-Aloud

- 我愛學中文。
  I love to learn Chinese.

- 也愛看中文書。
  (I) also love to read Chinese books.

- 可是黃狗把我的書吃了。
  But the yellow dog ate my books.

- 我看見了以後好生氣。
  I got really angry after I saw it.

- 只好出去玩了。
  (I) can only go out to play.

恭喜你完成了這一課,請回到第一頁將本課的愛心塗上顏色。
Congratulations! You have completed a lesson. Please color the heart for this lesson on page 1.

第十二課

Lesson 12 Běn – origin; classifier for books

本書中的國字筆順是依據中華民國教育部「常用國字標準字體筆順學習網」的筆劃順序彙編。
The stroke orders of the characters in this workbook follow the stroke orders provided on the "Learning Program for Stroke Order of Frequently Used Chinese Characters" website of the Ministry of Education, R.O.C. (Taiwan).

47

請將下方的字格剪下來讓孩子選擇正確的字貼上。
Please cut out the characters at the bottom and paste the correct ones.

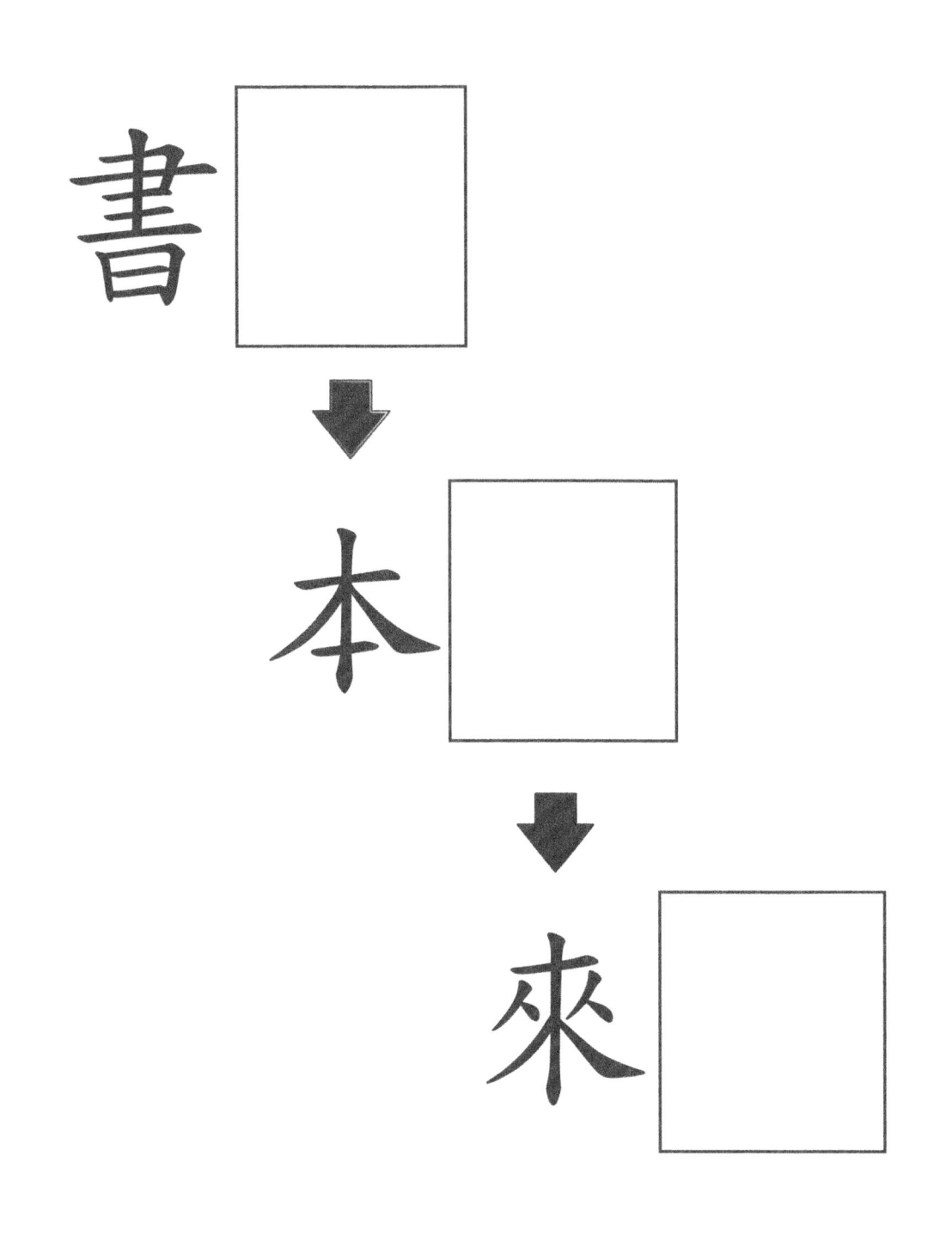

書 ☐

↓

本 ☐

↓

來 ☐

| 回 | 大 | 本 | 太 | 來 |

48

請依照下方指示將圖案著色。

Please color the picture according to the following:

書-黃色(yellow)
本-紅色(red)

唸唸看
Read-Aloud

- 我的書本為什麼不見了？
Why is my book gone?

- 媽媽說：「小黃狗又把書本吃了。」
Mom says, "The little yellow dog ate (your) book again."

- 我問：「他吃了幾本中文書？」
I ask, "How many Chinese books did it eat?"

- 媽媽說：「他吃了二十五本書。」
Mom says, "It ate twenty-five books."

- 我說：「真是的。」
I say, "Geez."

恭喜你完成了這一課，請回到第一頁將本課的愛心塗上顏色。
Congratulations! You have completed a lesson. Please color the heart for this lesson on page 1.

第十三課

Lesson 13 Chē – car

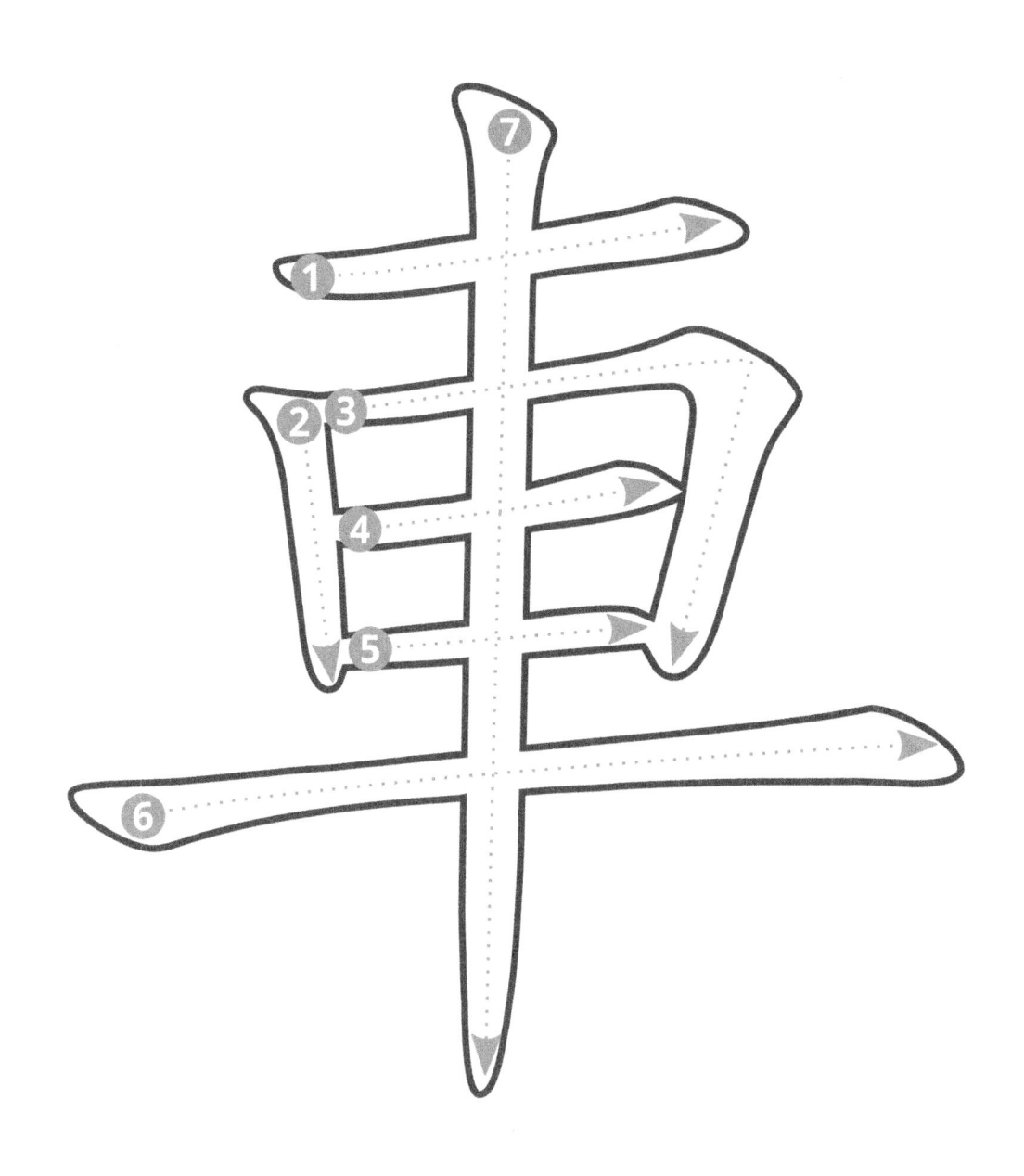

本書中的國字筆順是依據中華民國教育部「常用國字標準字體筆順學習網」的筆劃順序彙編。
The stroke orders of the characters in this workbook follow the stroke orders provided on the "Learning Program for Stroke Order of Frequently Used Chinese Characters" website of the Ministry of Education, R.O.C. (Taiwan).

「車」是象形字，它是由畜力車的樣子演變而來。
The character 車 is a pictograph. It looks like a cart.

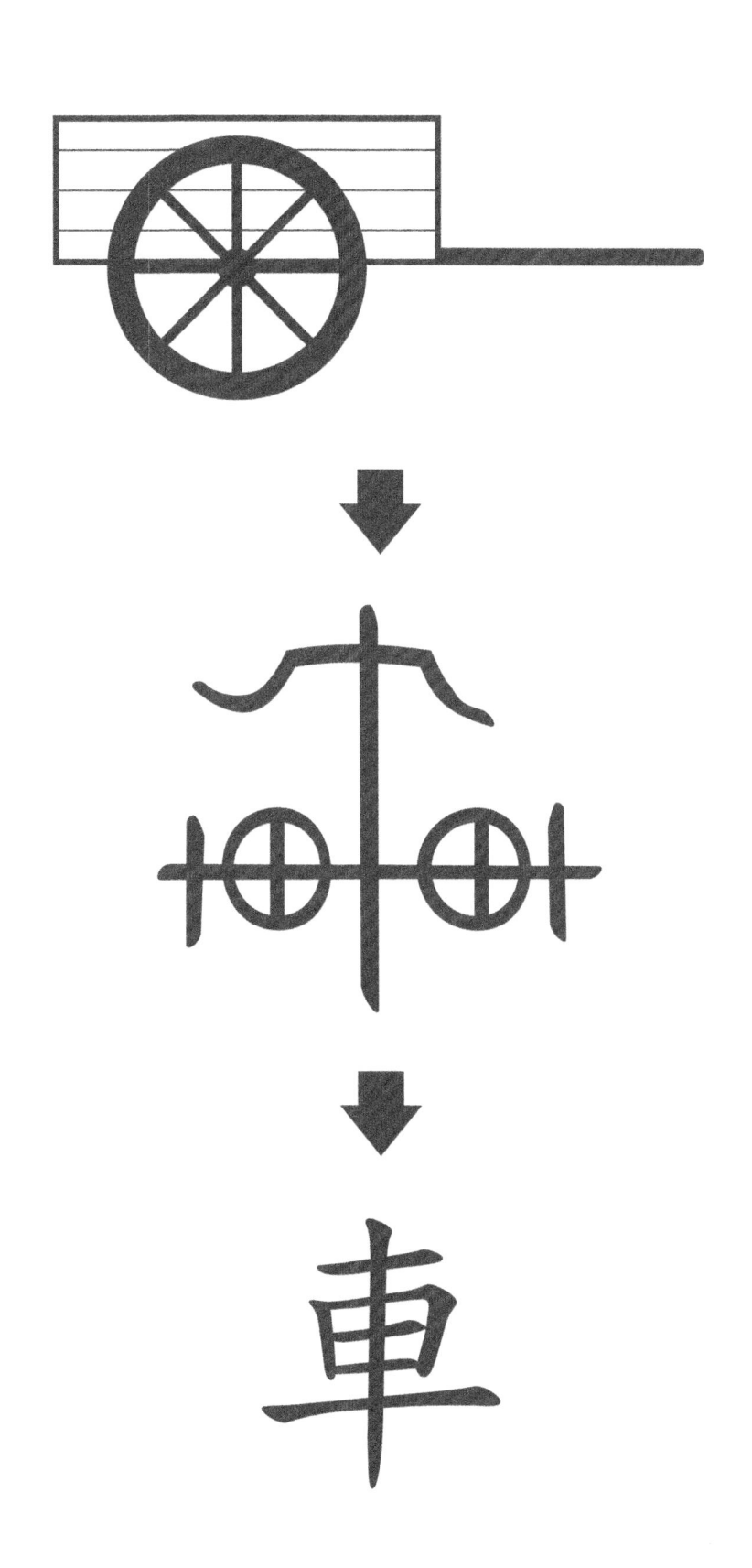

52

請圈出車子的圖案並唸出下方的文字。
Please circle the pictures of a car and read aloud the characters at the bottom.

車子在路上跑

唸唸看
Read-Aloud

- 老太太愛在車上看書。
  The old lady loves to read on the car.

- 他在車上看了三本中文書。
  She read three Chinese books on the car.

- 他下車前把書給了我。
  Before she got off the car, (she) gave me the books.

- 媽媽說不可以在車上看書。
  Mom says (I) can't read on the car.

- 我看書看得很快。
  I read books very fast.

恭喜你完成了這一課,請回到第一頁將本課的愛心塗上顏色。
Congratulations! You have completed a lesson. Please color the heart for this lesson on page 1.

第十四課

Lesson 14 Bā – eight

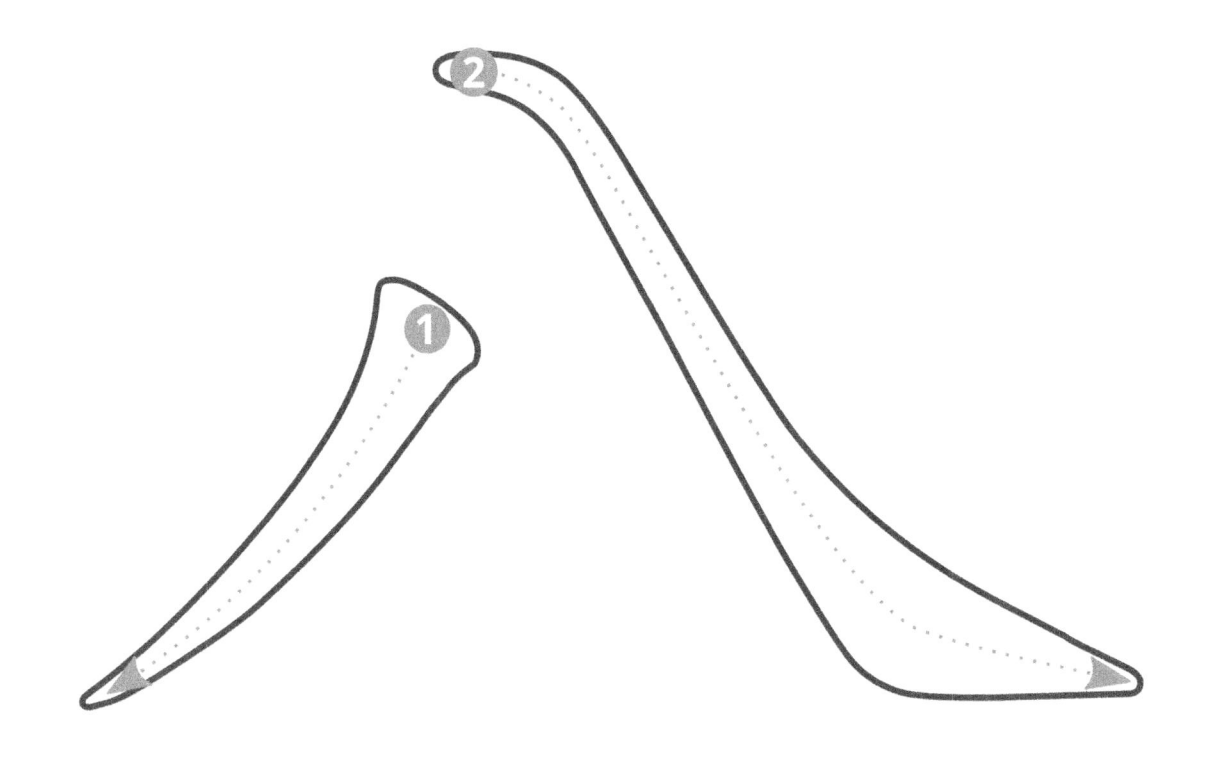

本書中的國字筆順是依據中華民國教育部「常用國字標準字體筆順學習網」的筆劃順序彙編。
The stroke orders of the characters in this workbook follow the stroke orders provided on the "Learning Program for Stroke Order of Frequently Used Chinese Characters" website of the Ministry of Education, R.O.C. (Taiwan).

連連看
Please connect the dots to complete the picture.

55

請將三個相同的物品連成一線。
Please connect the same items to win the tic-tac-toe.

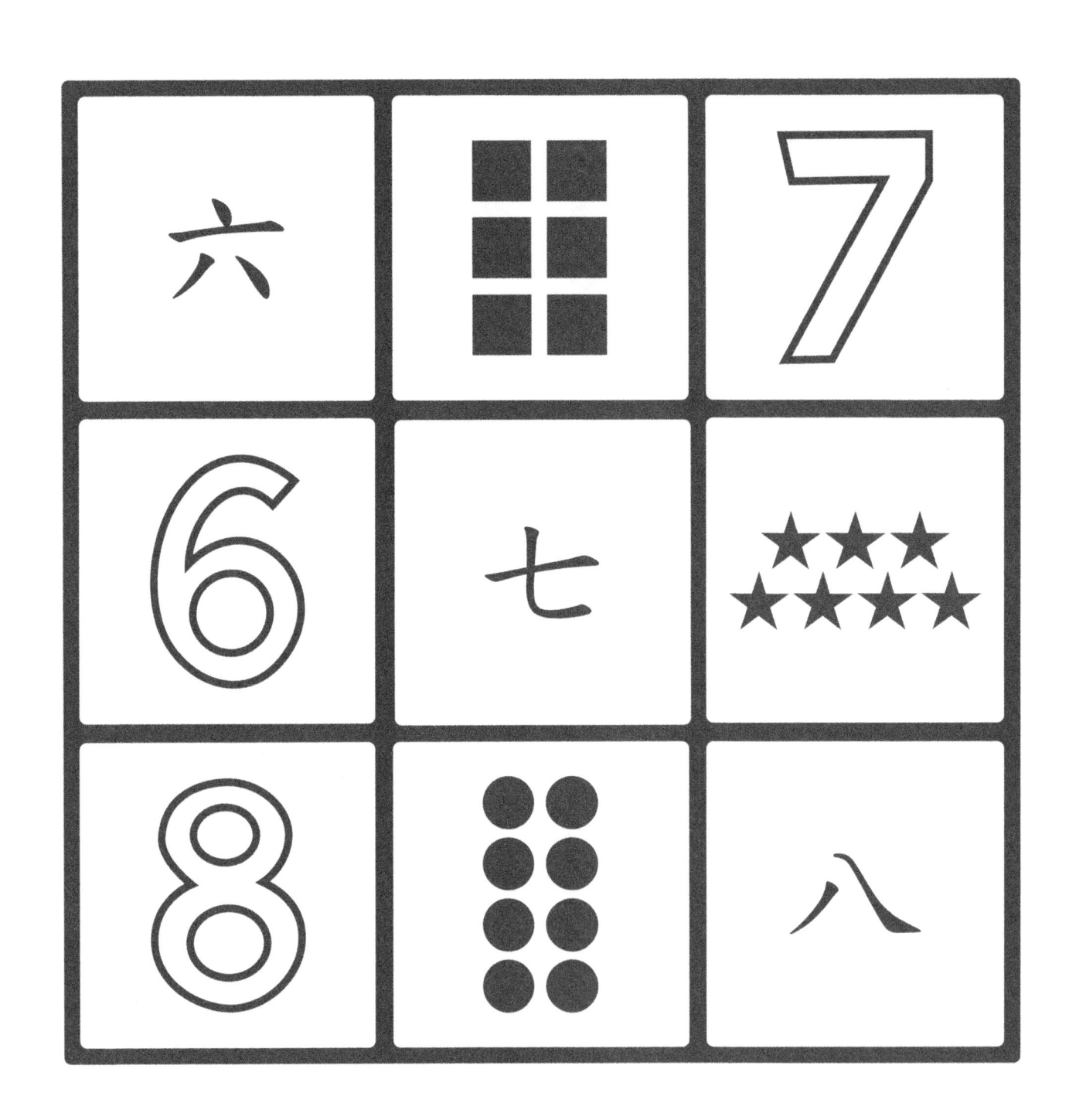

唸唸看
Read-Aloud

- 我愛作文也愛看書。
  I love to write essays and also love to read books.

- 我愛看中文書。
  I love to read Chinese books.

- 我看過八本書。
  I read eight books.

- 爸爸愛看車子的書。
  Dad loves to read books about cars.

- 他也看了八本書。
  He also read eight books.

恭喜你完成了這一課,請回到第一頁將本課的愛心塗上顏色。
Congratulations! You have completed a lesson. Please color the heart for this lesson on page 1.

第十五課

Lesson 15 Suǒ – place; that which

本書中的國字筆順是依據中華民國教育部「常用國字標準字體筆順學習網」的筆劃順序彙編。
The stroke orders of the characters in this workbook follow the stroke orders provided on the "Learning Program for Stroke Order of Frequently Used Chinese Characters" website of the Ministry of Education, R.O.C. (Taiwan).

請將下方的字格剪下來讓孩子選擇正確的字貼上。
Please cut out the characters at the bottom and paste the correct one.

戶 + 斤 = ☐

尸　戶　所　斤　斥

60

請圈出兩把完全一樣的雨傘。
Please circle the two identical umbrelllas.

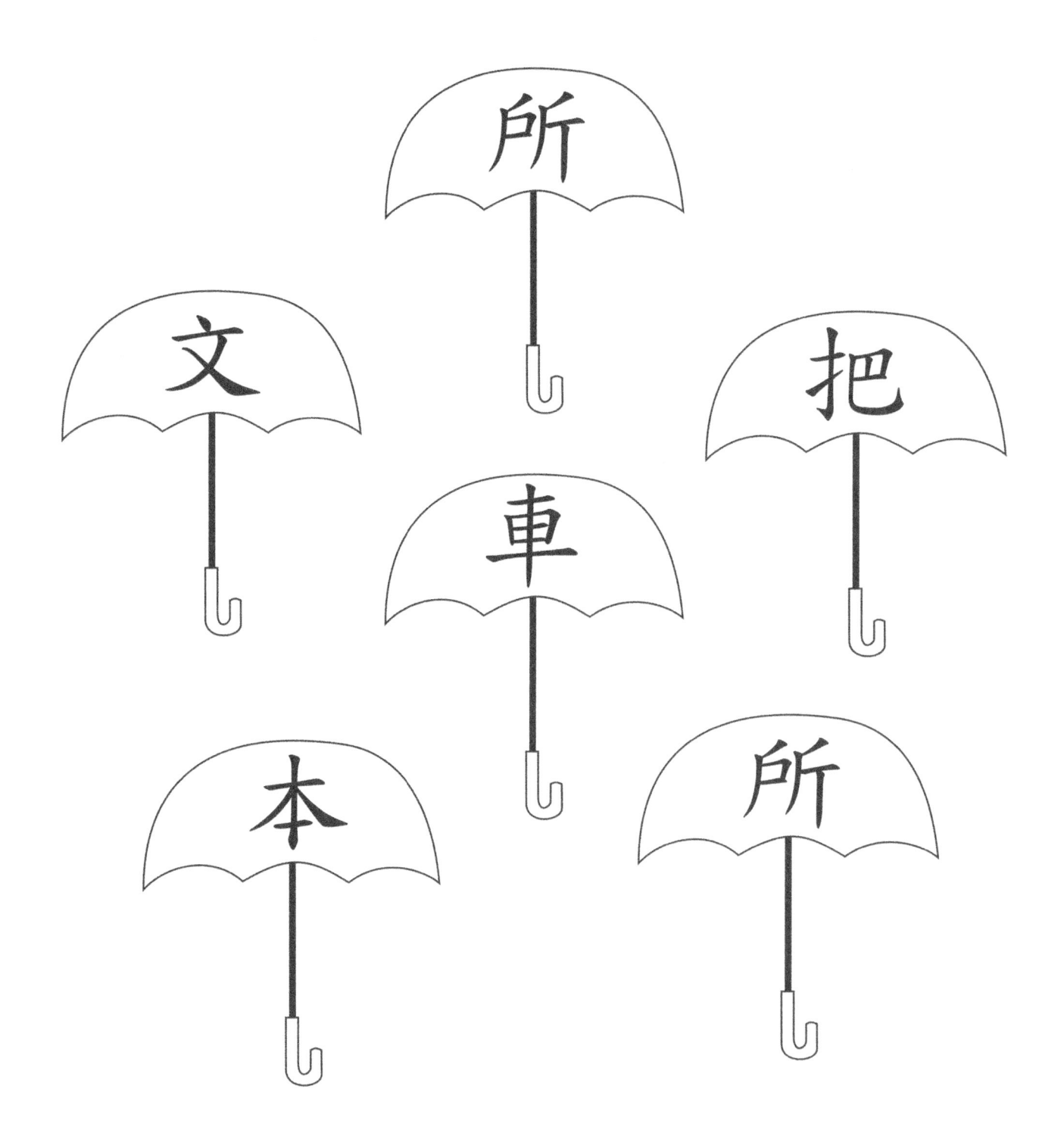

唸唸看
Read-Aloud

- 我看過八本很長的書。
I read eight very long books.

- 也會看大人的書。
(I) also read grown-up's books.

- 所以我很會作文。
Therefore, I am good at writing essays.

- 媽媽說不要在車上看書。
Mom says not to read books on the car.

- 所以我下車後看書。
Therefore, I read after (I) get off the car.

恭喜你完成了這一課,請回到第一頁將本課的愛心塗上顏色。
Congratulations! You have completed a lesson. Please color the heart for this lesson on page 1.

62

第十六課

Lesson 16 Xiě – to write

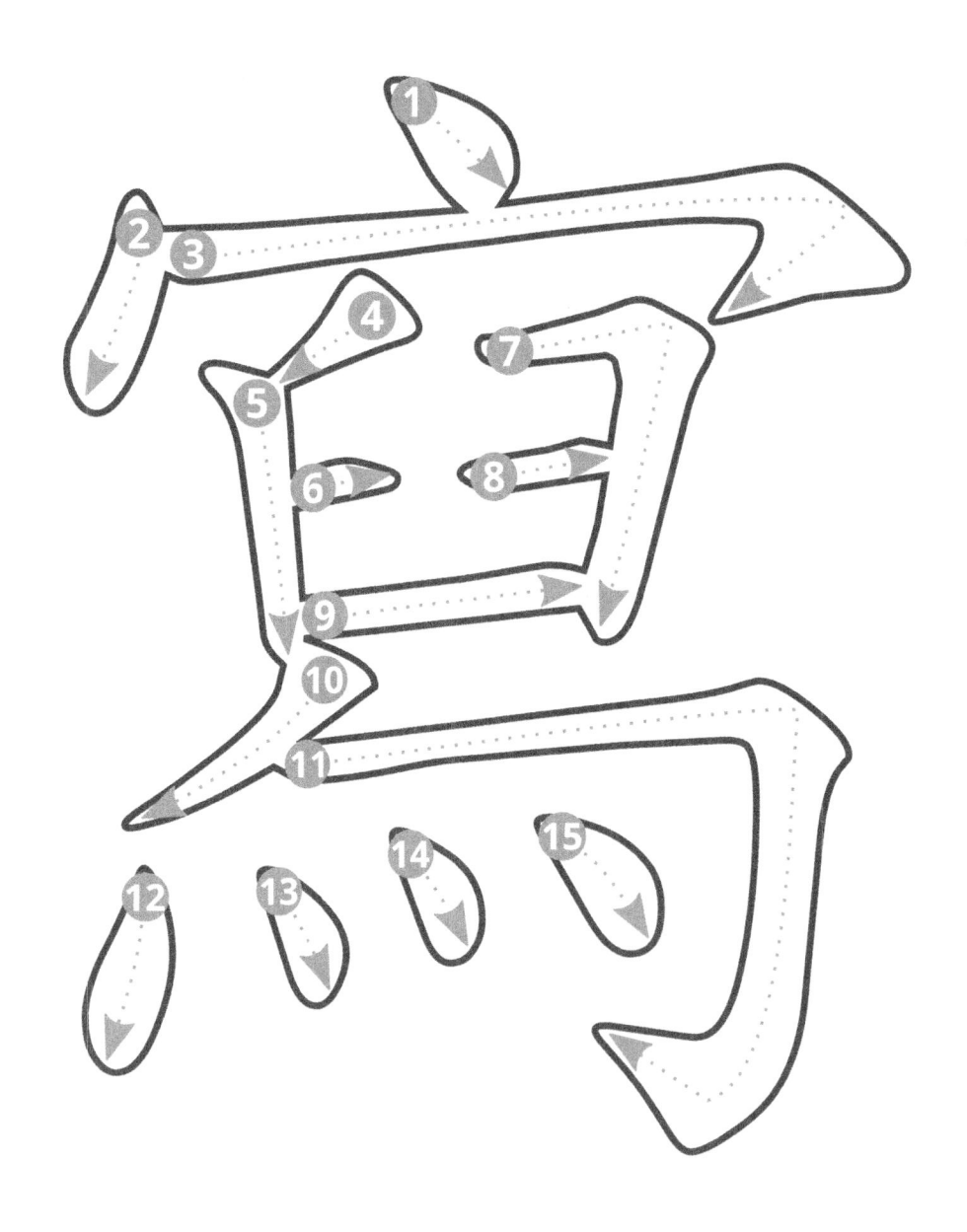

本書中的國字筆順是依據中華民國教育部「常用國字標準字體筆順學習網」的筆劃順序彙編。
The stroke orders of the characters in this workbook follow the stroke orders provided on the "Learning Program for Stroke Order of Frequently Used Chinese Characters" website of the Ministry of Education, R.O.C. (Taiwan).

請圈出寫字時需要用到的文具並唸出下方的文字。
Please circle the stationaries that are needed for writing and read aloud the characters below.

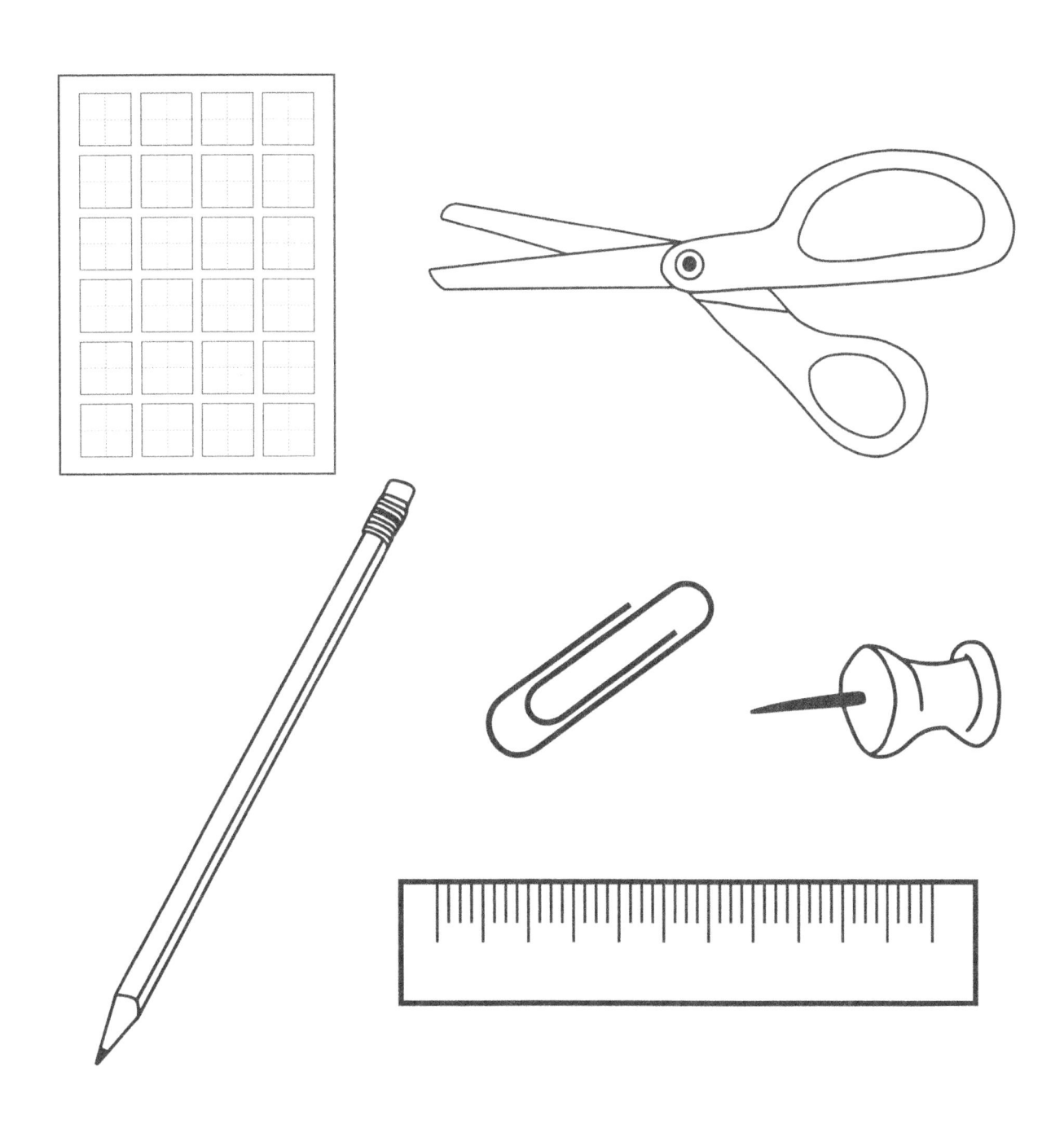

我愛寫作

64

請依照下方指示將圖案著色。
Please color the picture according to the following:

我－紅色(red)
愛－灰色(gray)
寫－黃色(yellow)
作－淺咖啡色(light brown)

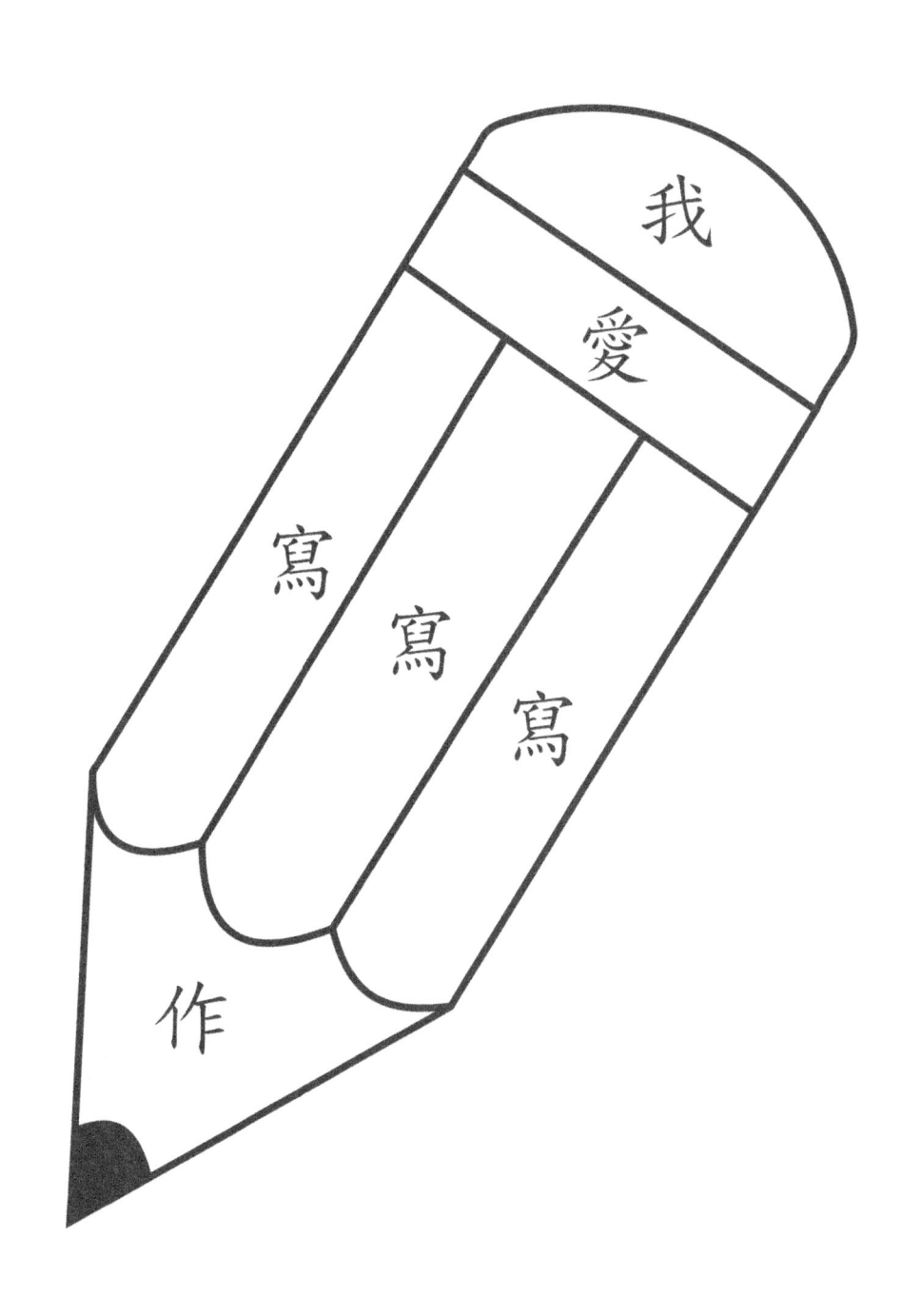

唸唸看
Read-Aloud

- 爸爸開車去工作。
  Dad drives to work.

- 我在家裡看了四十八本書。
  I read forty-eight books at home.

- 所以我作文寫得很好。
  Therefore, I am good at writing essays.

- 我以後要寫很多書。
  I want to write many books in the future.

恭喜你完成了這一課,請回到第一頁將本課的愛心塗上顏色。
Congratulations! You have completed a lesson. Please color the heart for this lesson on page 1.

第十七課

Lesson 17 Shì – thing; matter

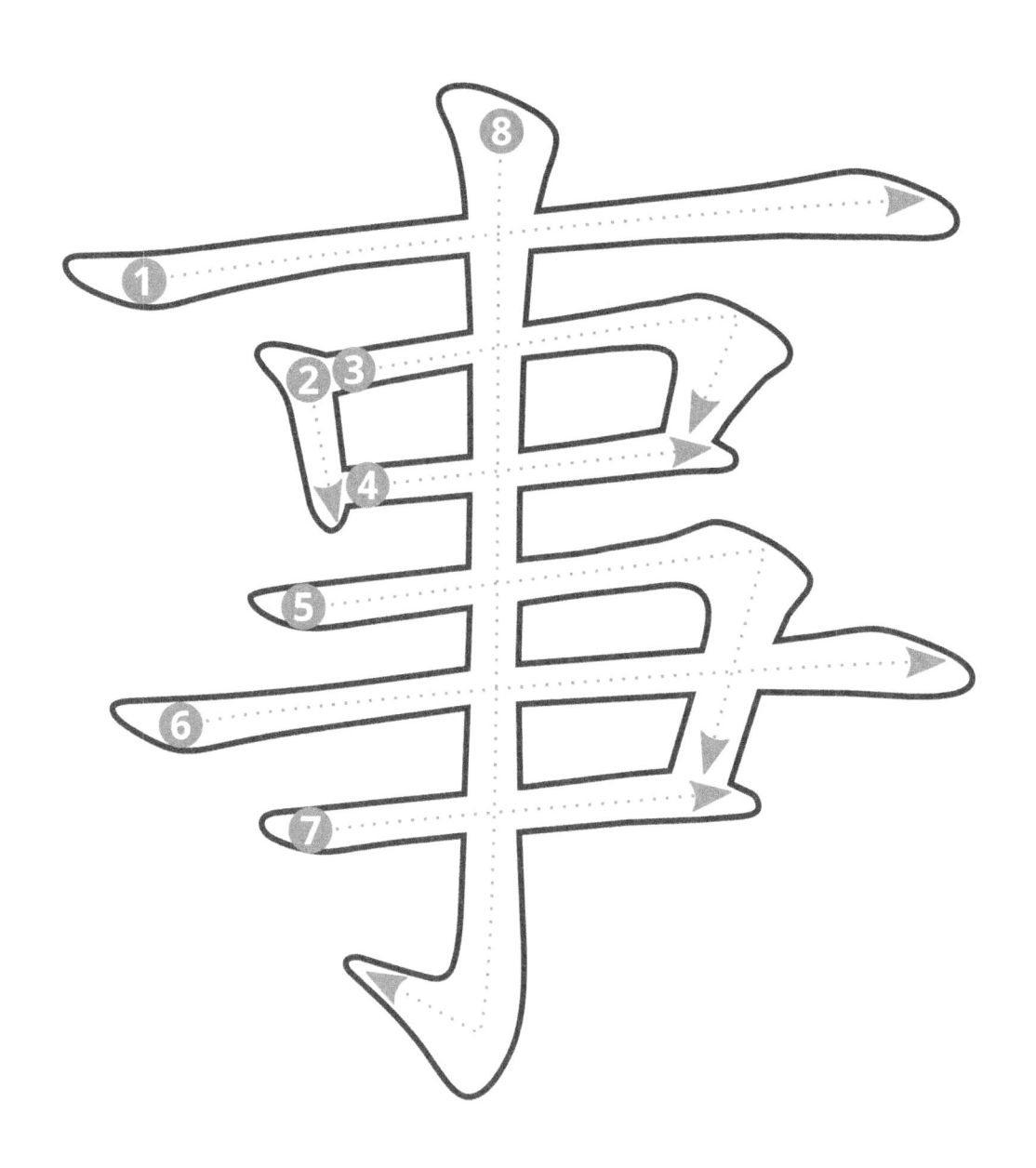

本書中的國字筆順是依據中華民國教育部「常用國字標準字體筆順學習網」的筆劃順序彙編。
The stroke orders of the characters in this workbook follow the stroke orders provided on the "Learning Program for Stroke Order of Frequently Used Chinese Characters" website of the Ministry of Education, R.O.C. (Taiwan).

找到「事」字圈出來。
Find the characters 事 and circle them.

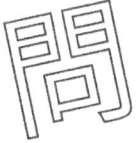

寫

事　　　事

　　本

　　問　　八

把　　　　車

事　　文　　事

　　書　　　問

請依照下方指示將圖案著色。
Please color the picture according to the following:

什－紅色(red)
麼－藍色(blue)
事－黃色(yellow)

唸唸看
Read-Aloud

- 明天沒有事，所以我們會開車出去玩。
  Tomorrow (we) have nothing to do, therefore, we will drive out to play.

- 我們會去高山上玩。
  We will go play in the high mountains.

- 天空上有八朵白雲。
  There are eight clouds in the sky.

- 山上的空氣很好。
  The air on the mountain is very good (fresh and clear).

- 我會把出去玩的事寫下來。
  I will write about my trip out to play.

恭喜你完成了這一課，請回到第一頁將本課的愛心塗上顏色。
Congratulations! You have completed a lesson. Please color the heart for this lesson on page 1.

第十八課

Lesson 18 Gù – happening; old

本書中的國字筆順是依據中華民國教育部「常用國字標準字體筆順學習網」的筆劃順序彙編。
The stroke orders of the characters in this workbook follow the stroke orders provided on the "Learning Program for Stroke Order of Frequently Used Chinese Characters" website of the Ministry of Education, R.O.C. (Taiwan).

請將下方的字格剪下來讓孩子選擇正確的字貼上。
Please cut out the characters at the bottom and paste the correct one.

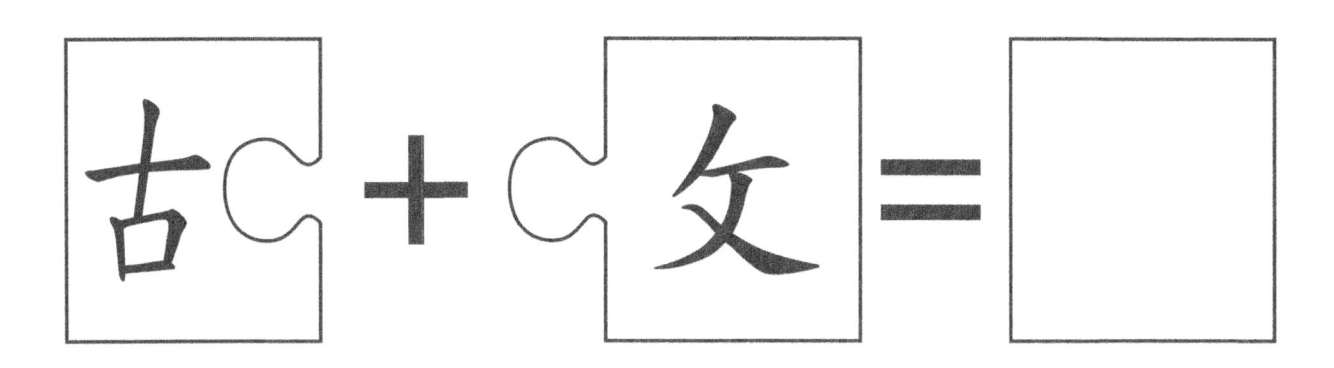

古 + 攵 = ☐

| 故 | 古 | 牧 | 啟 | 攵 |

請將有「故」字的地方著色。
Color the areas with the character 故.

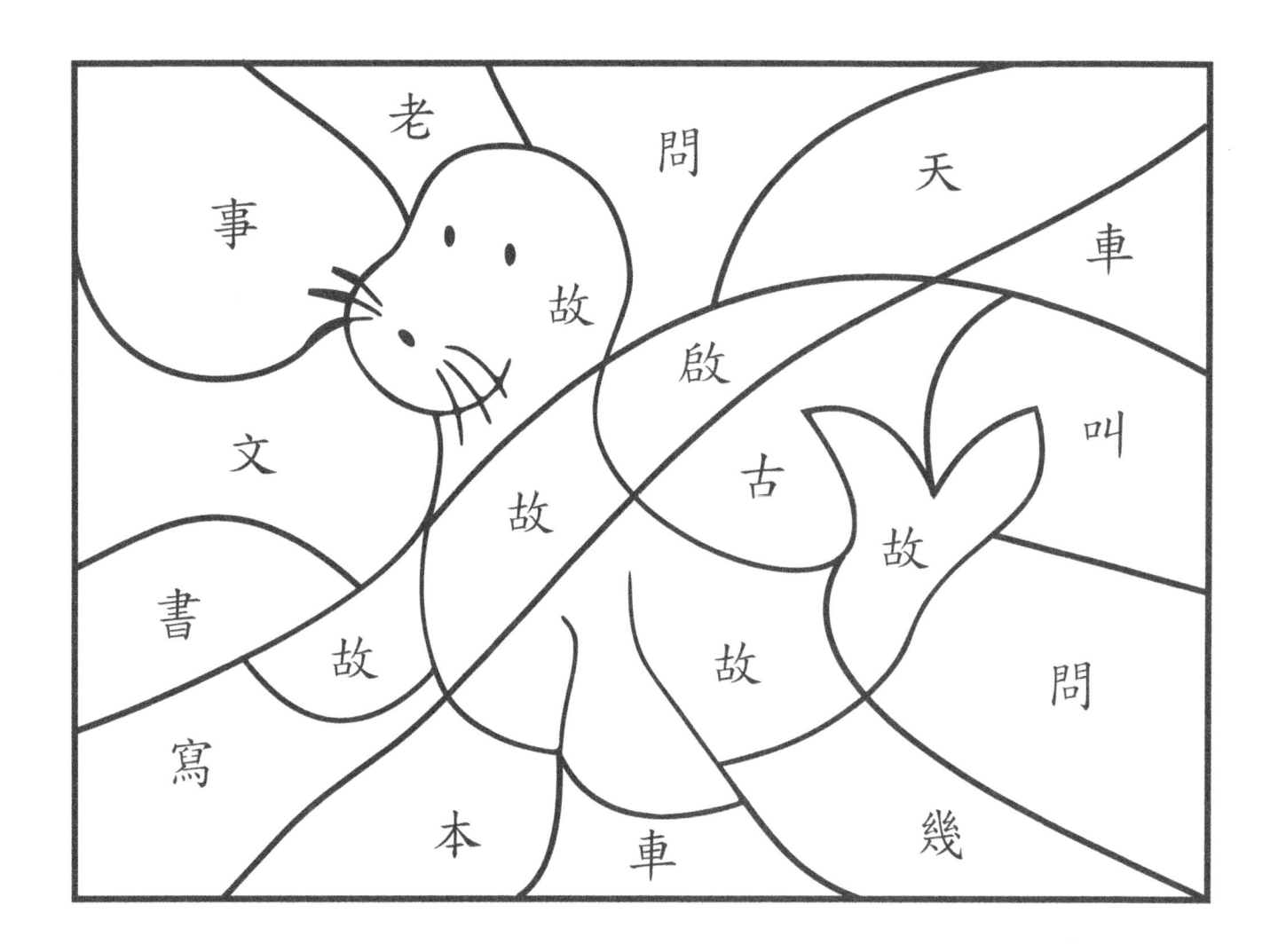

唸唸看
Read-Aloud

- 有一天我寫了一個故事。
  One day, I wrote a story.

- 從前有一隻耳朵很長的兔子在土地上跳。
  Once upon a time, there was a rabbit with very long ears hopping on the ground.

- 他跳了八十下還是跳不到樹上。
  He hopped for eighty times, but he still cannot hop onto the tree.

- 他說：「我還是在下頭就好了。」
  He said, "I shall remain down here."

- 你說這個故事好不好聽？
  Do you think this story is good?

恭喜你完成了這一課，請回到第一頁將本課的愛心塗上顏色。
Congratulations! You have completed a lesson. Please color the heart for this lesson on page 1.

第十九課

Lesson 19 Cháng – often; frequently; constant

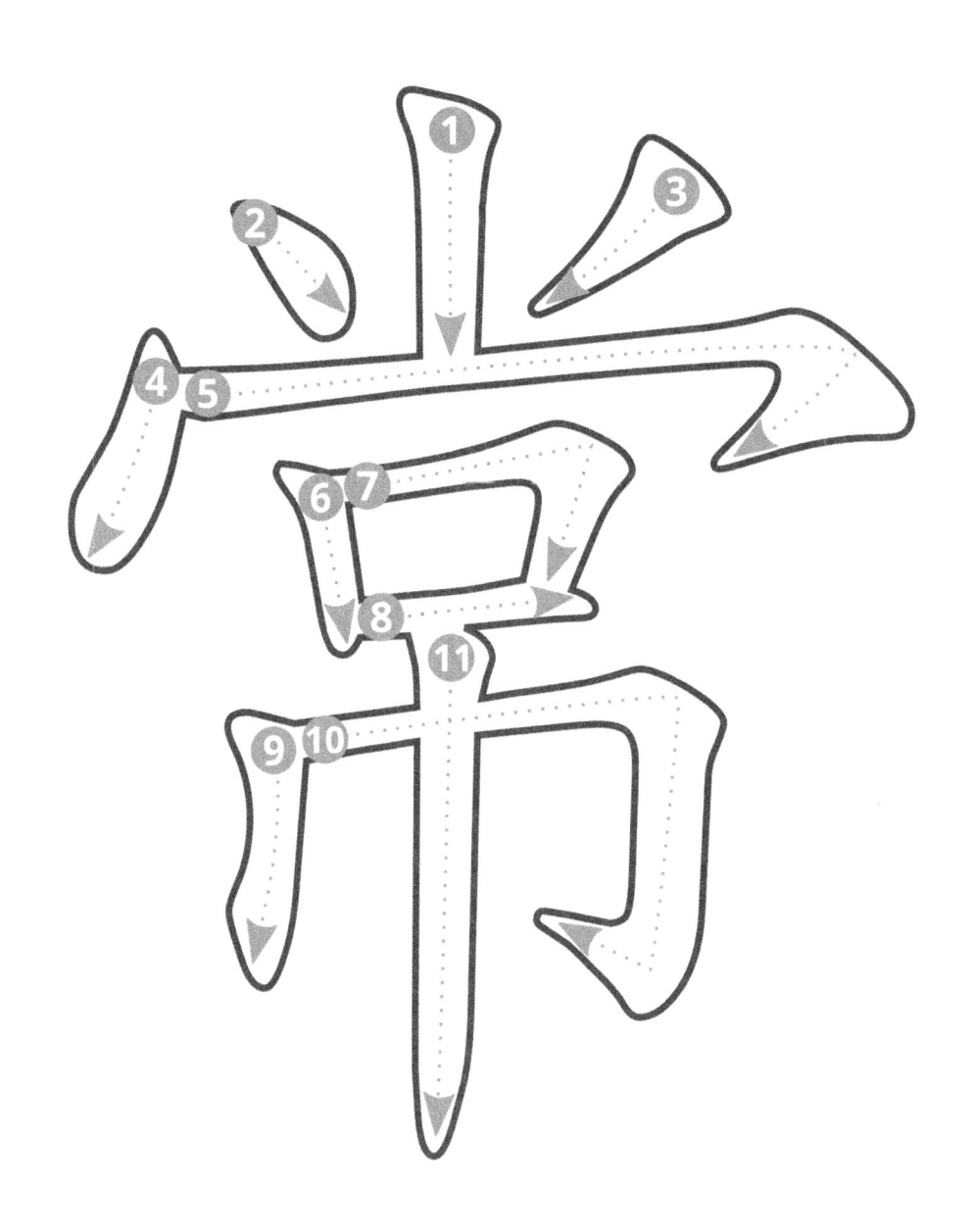

本書中的國字筆順是依據中華民國教育部「常用國字標準字體筆順學習網」的筆劃順序彙編。
The stroke orders of the characters in this workbook follow the stroke orders provided on the "Learning Program for Stroke Order of Frequently Used Chinese Characters" website of the Ministry of Education, R.O.C. (Taiwan).

75

將「常」字塗色，幫貓熊找到竹子。
Color the characters 常 to help the panda find the bamboos.

找出「常」字圈出來。
Find the characters 常 and circle them.

唸唸看
Read-Aloud

- 老太太常常說故事給我聽。
  The old lady often tells me stories.

- 小黃狗也愛和我一起聽。
  The little yellow dog also loves to listen with me.

- 可是他常常會吃故事書。
  But he often eat story books.

- 所以我要把所有的故事都寫下來。
  Therefore, I will wite down all the stories.

- 故事就不會不見了。
  (Then,) the stories will not be gone.

恭喜你完成了這一課,請回到第一頁將本課的愛心塗上顏色。
Congratulations! You have completed a lesson. Please color the heart for this lesson on page 1.

第二十課

Lesson 20 Dì – younger brother; junior male

本書中的國字筆順是依據中華民國教育部「常用國字標準字體筆順學習網」的筆劃順序彙編。
The stroke orders of the characters in this workbook follow the stroke orders provided on the "Learning Program for Stroke Order of Frequently Used Chinese Characters" website of the Ministry of Education, R.O.C. (Taiwan).

找到「弟」字圈出來。
Find the characters 弟 and circle them.

弟　本　　　　弟

　　問

　　　　　寫
弟
　　　車　　　弟

　　文　　常
把　　書

80

請將下圖著色並唸出下方文字。
Please color the picture and read aloud the characters below.

我愛弟弟

我是弟弟

請將下圖著色並唸出下方文字。
Please color the picture and read aloud the characters below.

唸唸看
Read-Aloud

- 弟弟常常在車上看故事書。
  (My) little brother often reads story books on the car.

- 我叫弟弟不要在車上看。
  I tell (my) little brother not to read on the car.

- 可是弟弟不聽話。
  But my little brother does not listen.

- 在車上看了好幾本書。
  (He) read several books on the car.

- 他也想要學會寫故事。
  He also wants to learn how to write stories.

恭喜你完成了這一課,請回到第一頁將本課的愛心塗上顏色。
Congratulations! You have completed a lesson. Please color the heart for this lesson on page 1.

第二十一課

Lesson 21 Jīng – to pass through

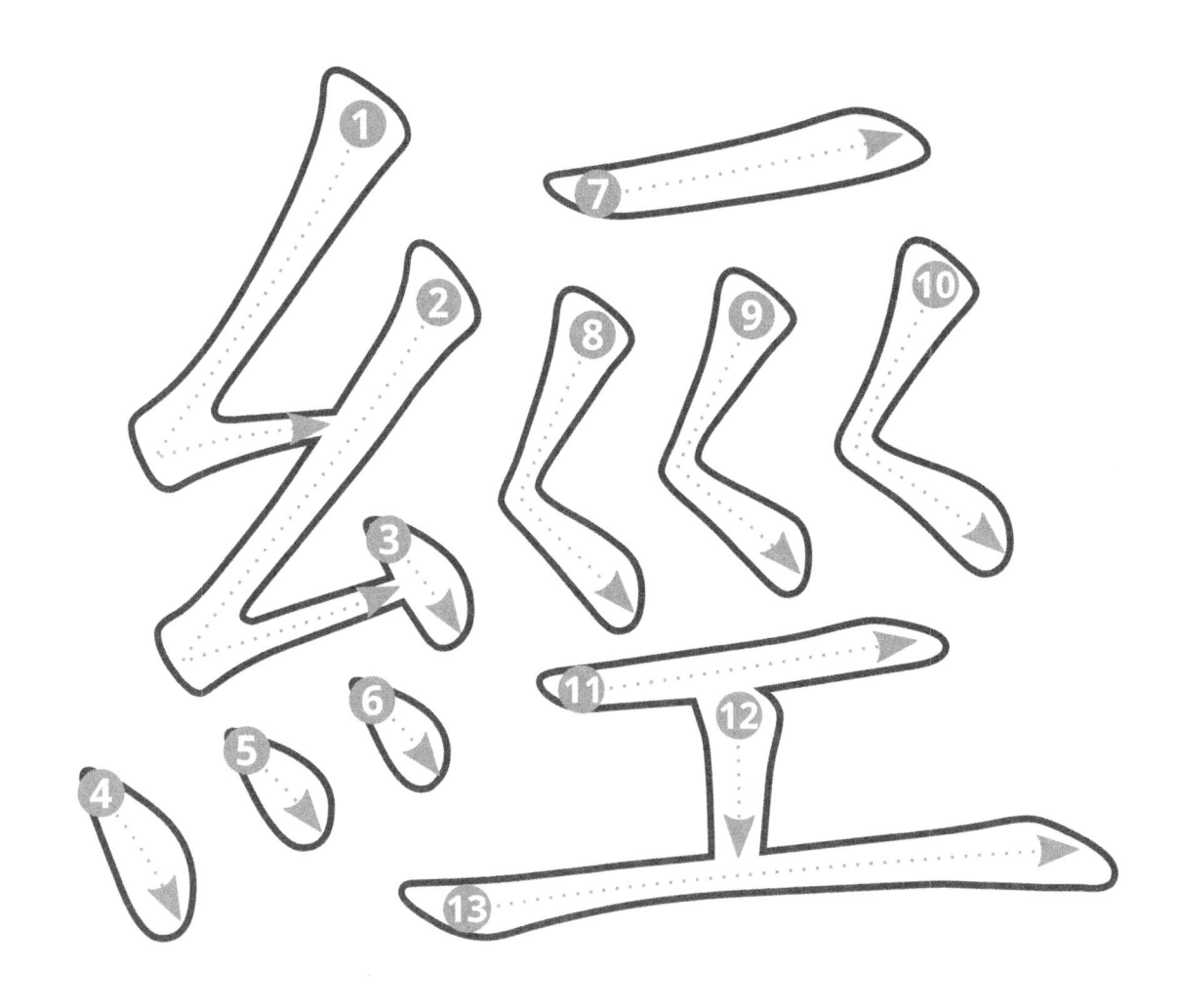

本書中的國字筆順是依據中華民國教育部「常用國字標準字體筆順學習網」的筆劃順序彙編。
The stroke orders of the characters in this workbook follow the stroke orders provided on the "Learning Program for Stroke Order of Frequently Used Chinese Characters" website of the Ministry of Education, R.O.C. (Taiwan).

請將下方的字格剪下來讓孩子選擇正確的字貼上。
Please cut out the characters at the bottom and paste the correct ones.

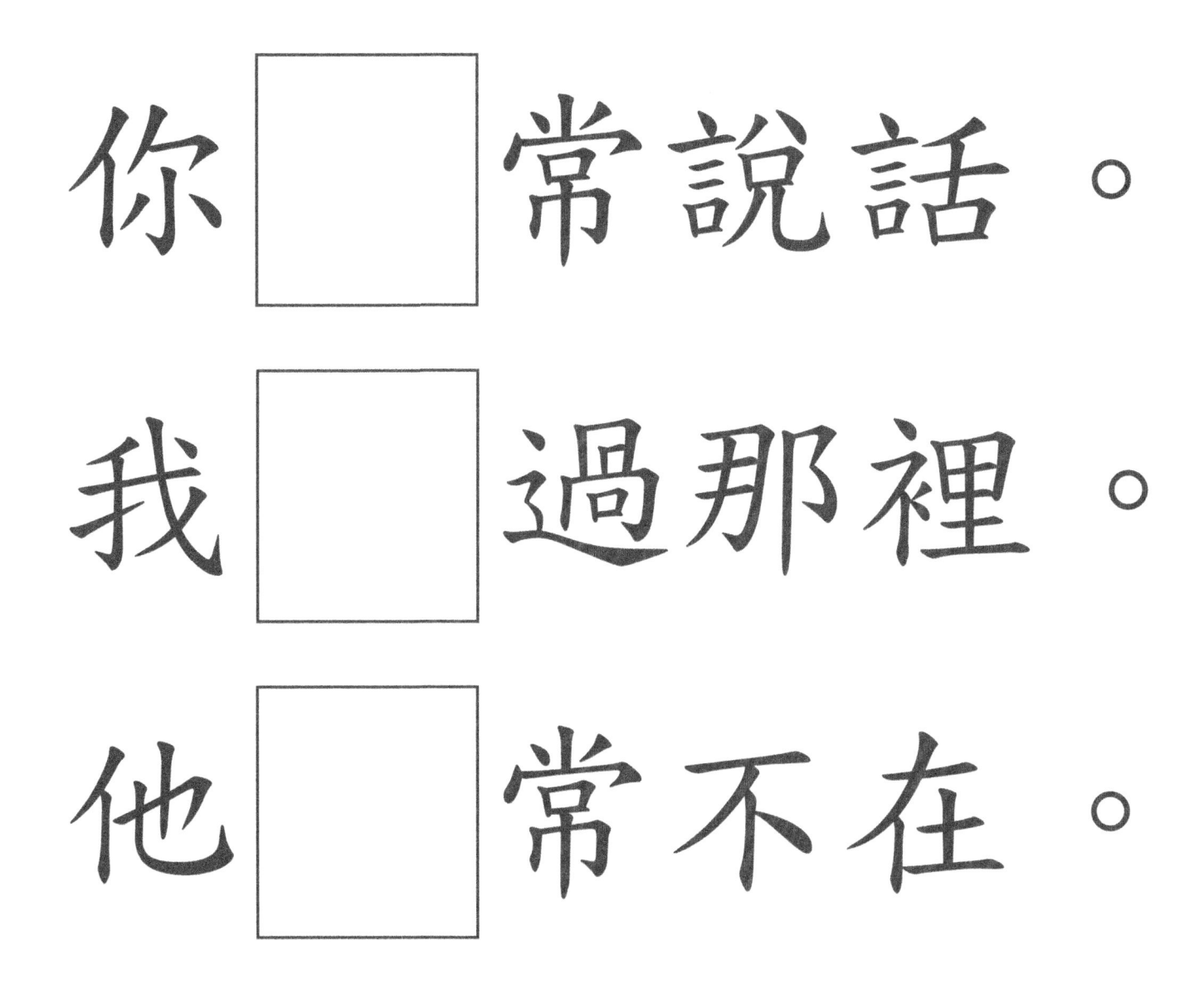

你☐常說話。

我☐過那裡。

他☐常不在。

| 經 | 輕 | 經 | 徑 | 經 |

84

跟著「經」字走幫助女孩走回家。
Please follow the character 經 to find the path home.

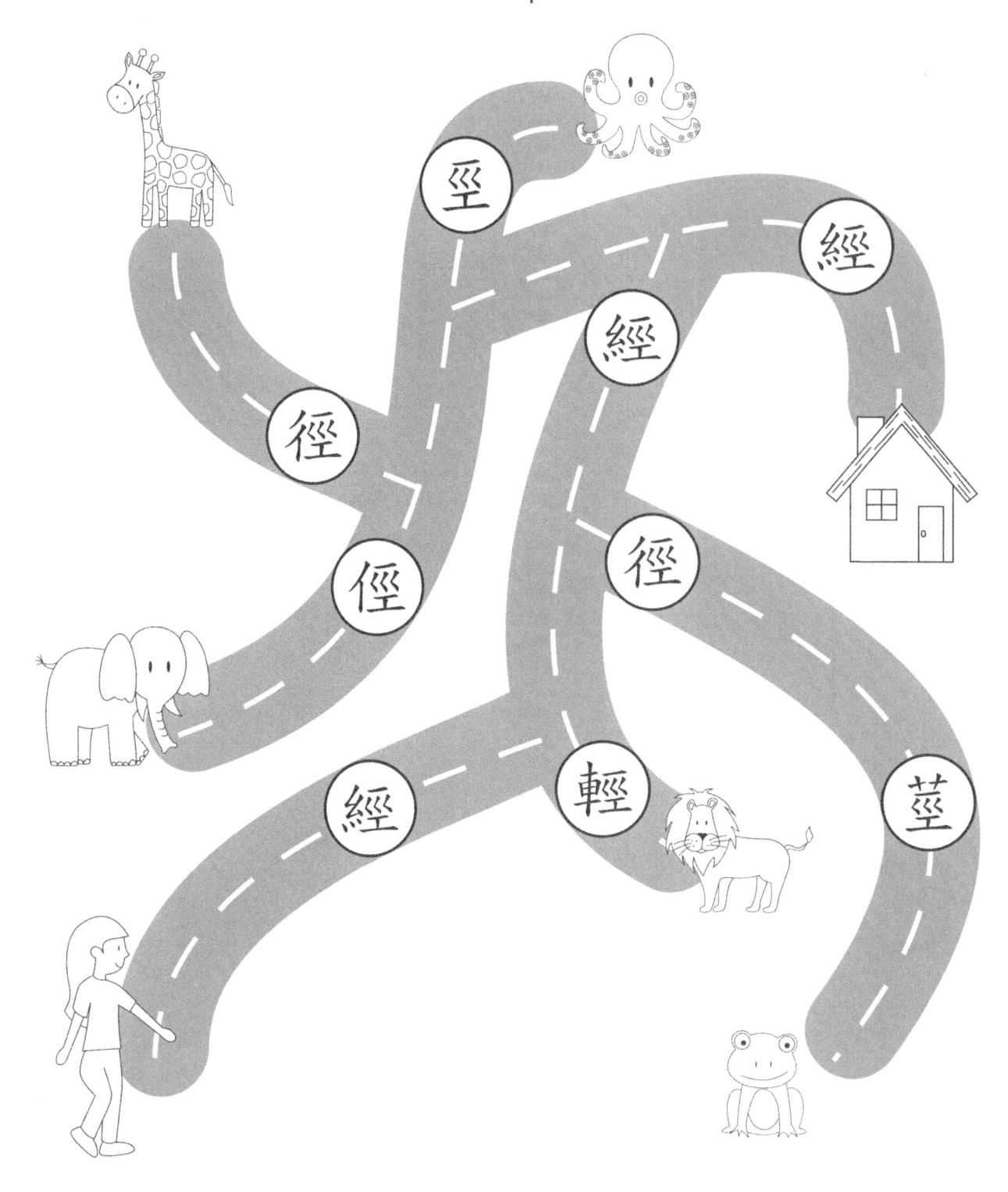

唸唸看
Read-Aloud

- 弟弟經常在車上看故事書。
  (My) little brother often reads story books on the car.

- 媽媽和他說不可以。
  Mom tells him not to.

- 弟弟會聽媽媽的話。
  (My) little brother will listen to Mom.

- 媽媽在車上說故事給弟弟聽。
  Mom tells stories to (my) little brother on the car.

- 車子經過了我們家。
  The car passed by our house.

恭喜你完成了這一課,請回到第一頁將本課的愛心塗上顏色。
Congratulations! You have completed a lesson. Please color the heart for this lesson on page 1.

第二十二課

Lesson 22 Yǐ – already

本書中的國字筆順是依據中華民國教育部「常用國字標準字體筆順學習網」的筆劃順序彙編。
The stroke orders of the characters in this workbook follow the stroke orders provided on the "Learning Program for Stroke Order of Frequently Used Chinese Characters" website of the Ministry of Education, R.O.C. (Taiwan).

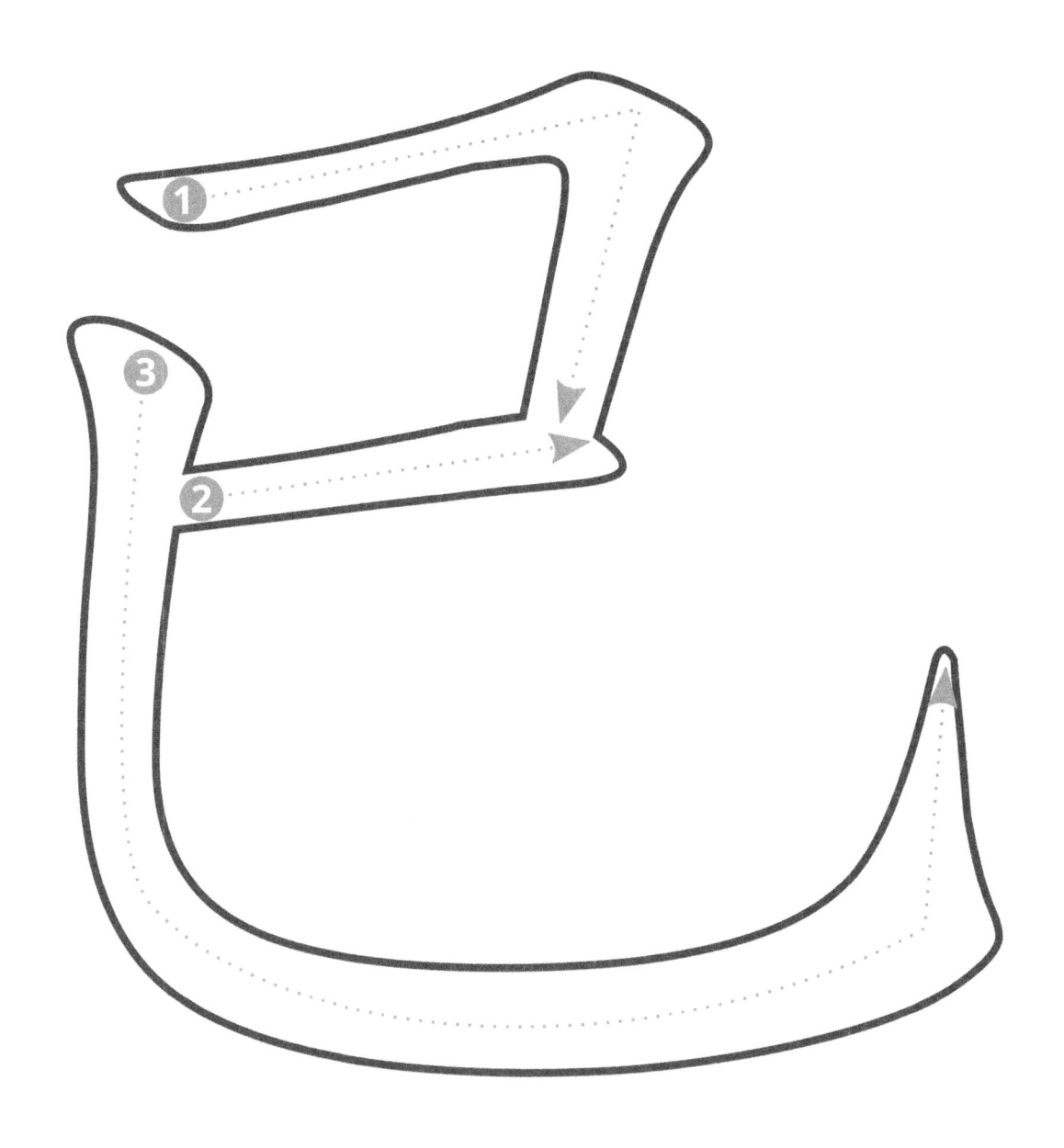

找出到達「已」字的路。
Find the path leading to the character 已.

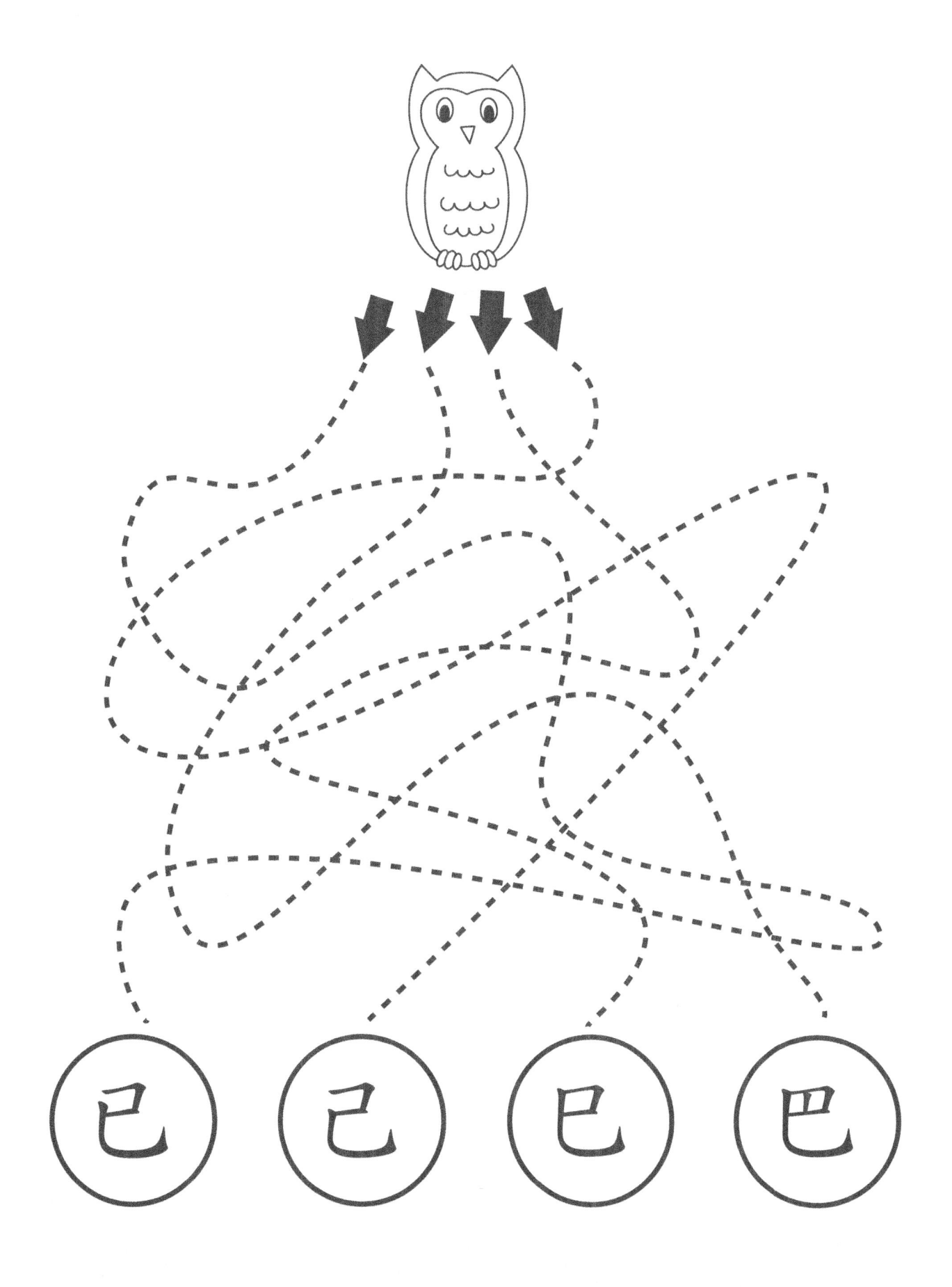

87

跟著「已」字從 ➡ 到 ★ 走出迷宮。
Follow the characters 已 from the arrow to the star to exit the maze.

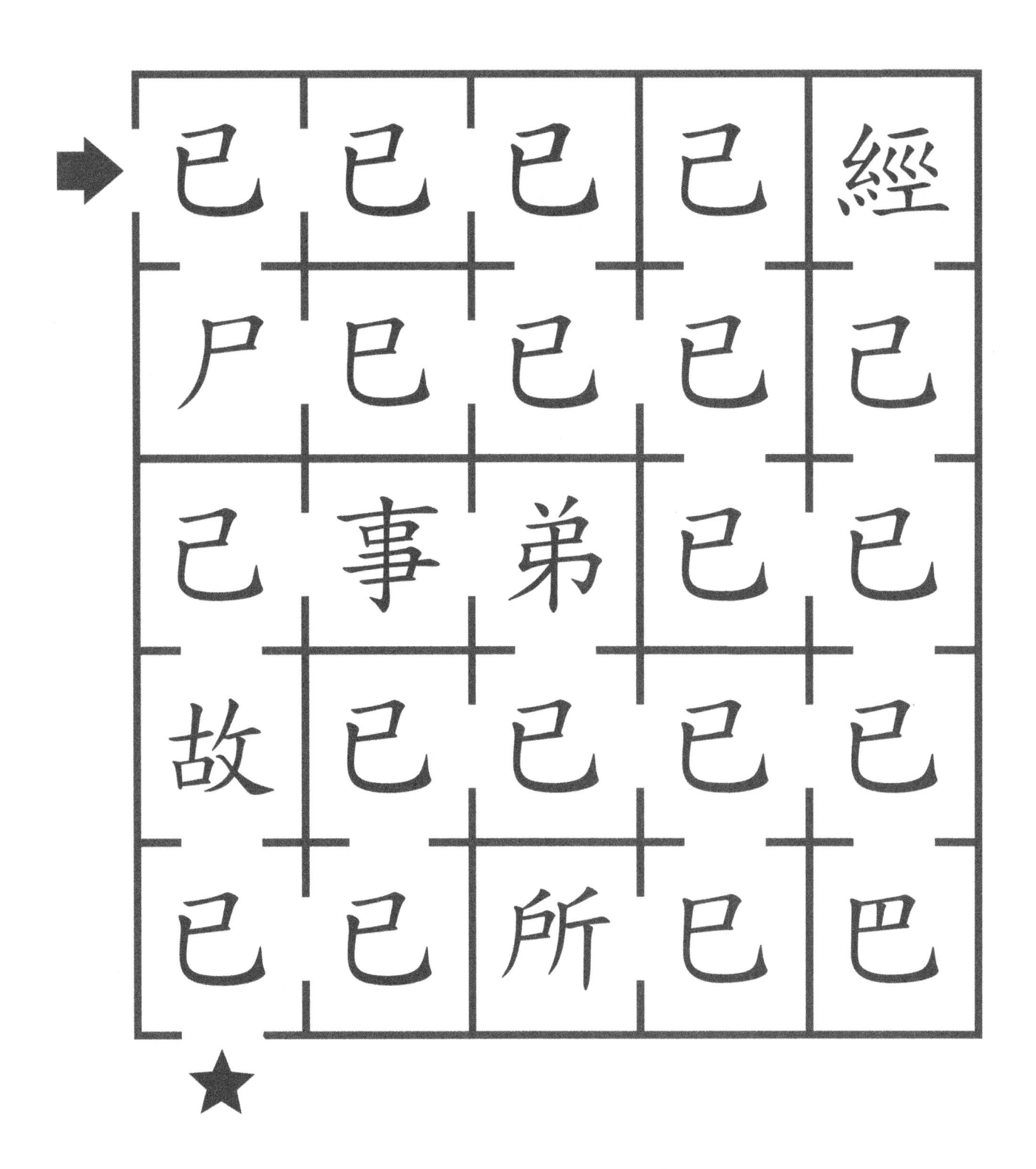

已	已	已	己	經
尸	巳	已	已	己
己	事	弟	已	已
故	已	已	已	已
已	已	所	巳	巴

唸唸看
Read-Aloud

- 老太太常常給小弟弟吃點心。
  The old lady often gives desserts to (my) little brother to eat.

- 又會說好多故事給他聽。
  (She) also tells him many stories.

- 小弟弟已經吃不下了。
  (My) little brother is already full.

- 小弟弟已經聽了所有的故事。
  (My) little brother already heard all the stories.

- 他真的很開心。
  He is really happy.

恭喜你完成了這一課，請回到第一頁將本課的愛心塗上顏色。
Congratulations! You have completed a lesson. Please color the heart for this lesson on page 1.

第二十三課

Lesson 23 Hēi – black; dark

本書中的國字筆順是依據中華民國教育部「常用國字標準字體筆順學習網」的筆劃順序彙編。
The stroke orders of the characters in this workbook follow the stroke orders provided on the "Learning Program for Stroke Order of Frequently Used Chinese Characters" website of the Ministry of Education, R.O.C. (Taiwan).

請把天空塗上黑色，月亮和星星塗上黃色，並念出下方的文字。
Please color the sky black, the moon and the stars yellow, and read aloud the characters at the bottom.

黑色的天空

92

連連看一樣的字。
Draw a line to the matching character.

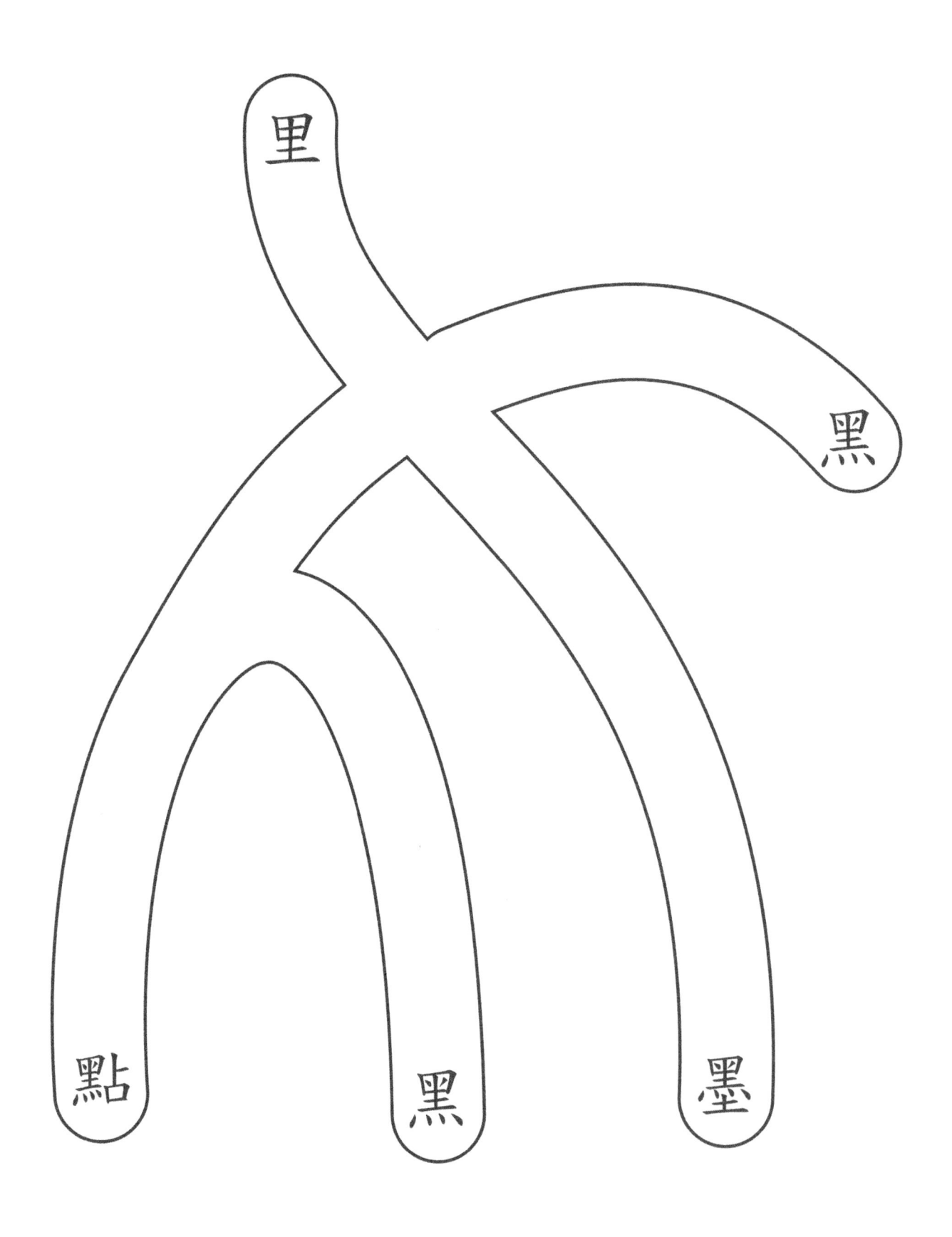

里　　　黑

點　　黑　　墨

唸唸看
Read-Aloud

- 天已經黑了。
  It's already dark.

- 可是弟弟還不想回家。
  But (my) little brother still does not want to go home.

- 媽媽和他說：「天黑了要回家，以後我們還是可以時常出來玩。」
  Mom tells him, "(Let's) go home (since) it's dark, we can still go out to play often in the future."

- 弟弟說：「好。」
  (My) little brother says, "Okay."

- 弟弟好聽話。
  (My) little brother is very obedient.

恭喜你完成了這一課，請回到第一頁將本課的愛心塗上顏色。
Congratulations! You have completed a lesson. Please color the heart for this lesson on page 1.

第二十四課

Lesson 24 Zài – again

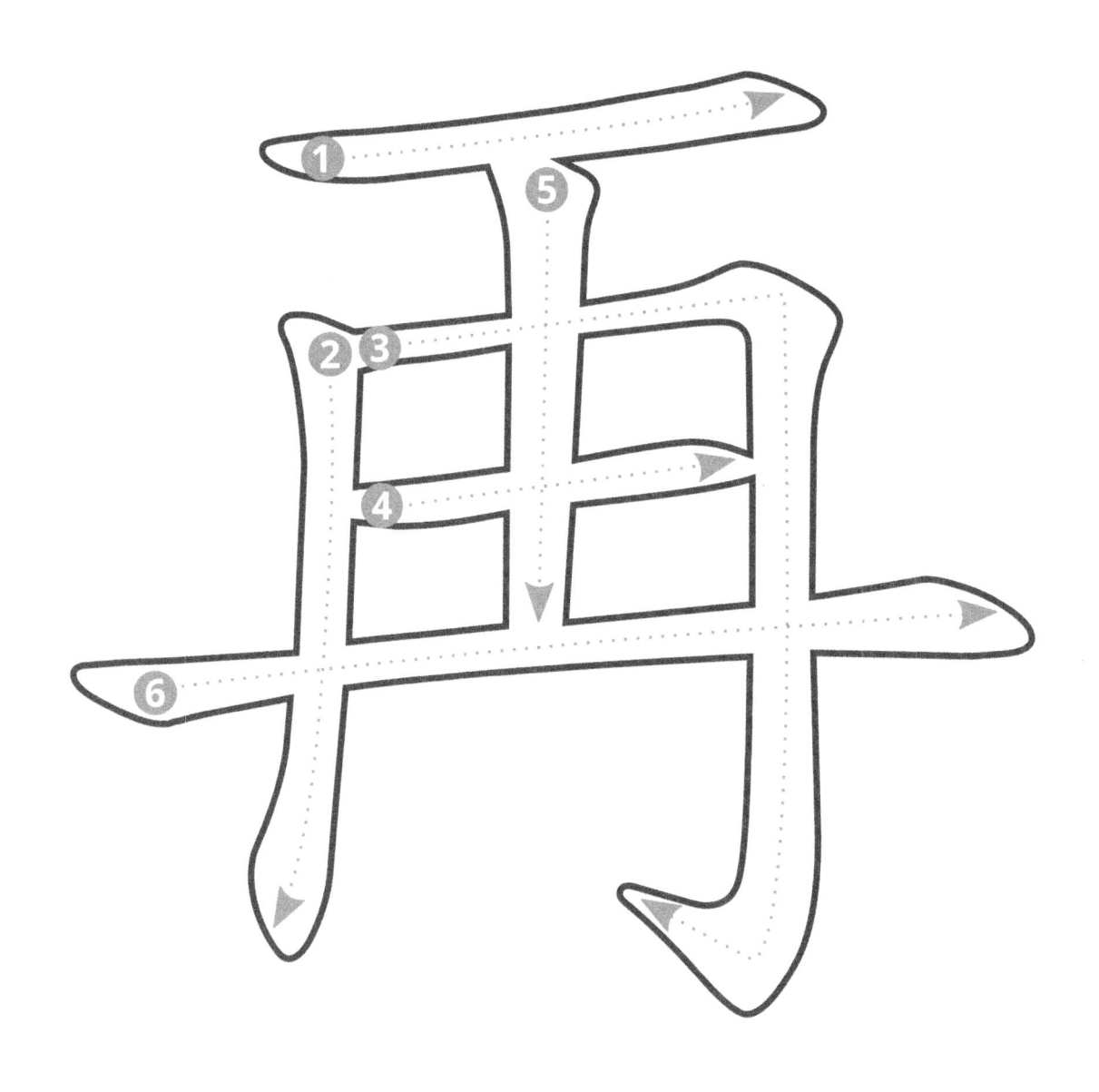

本書中的國字筆順是依據中華民國教育部「常用國字標準字體筆順學習網」的筆劃順序彙編。
The stroke orders of the characters in this workbook follow the stroke orders provided on the "Learning Program for Stroke Order of Frequently Used Chinese Characters" website of the Ministry of Education, R.O.C. (Taiwan).

連連看一樣的字。
Draw lines to connect the matching characters.

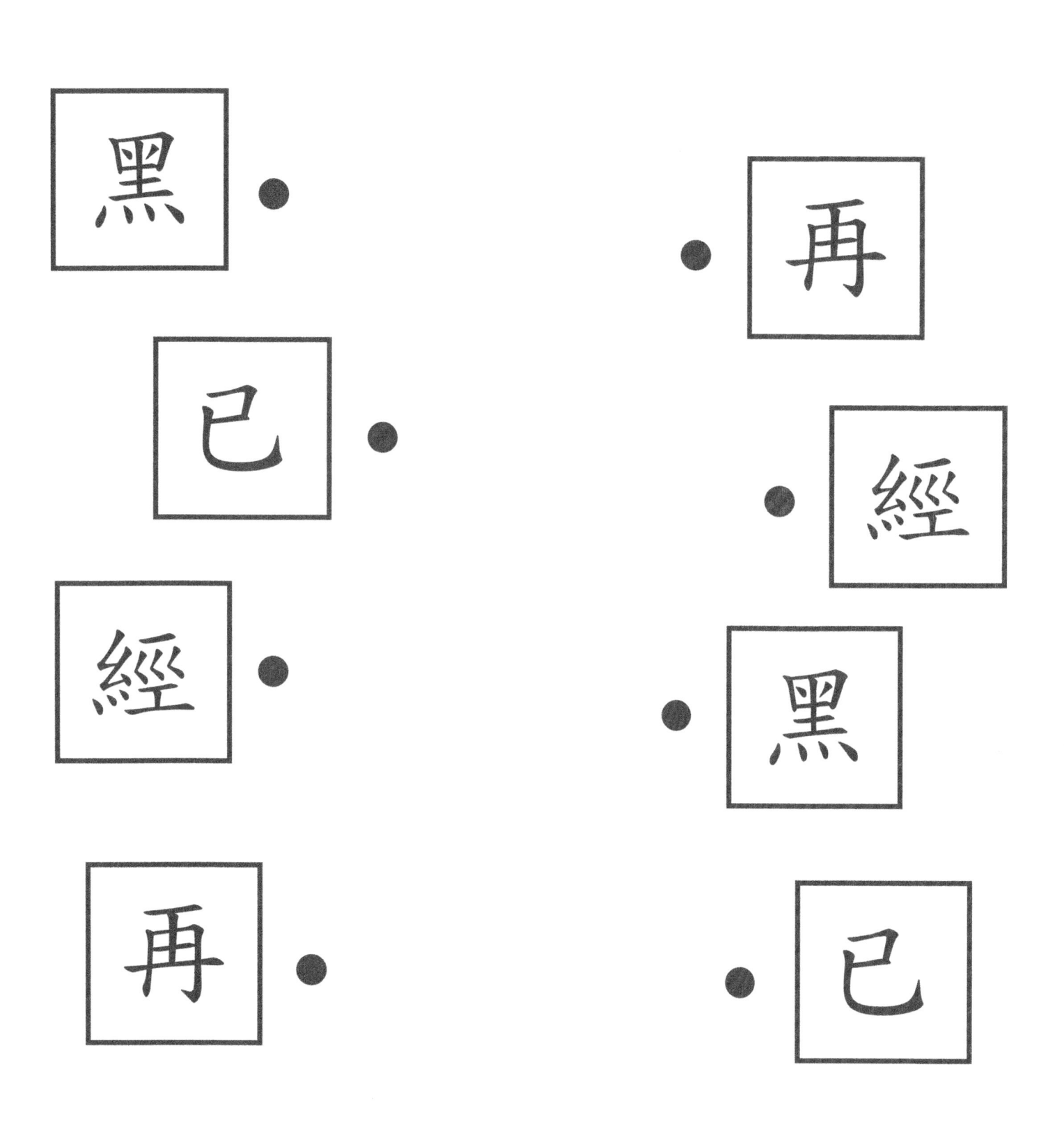

請圈出與圖案相對應的文字。
Circle the phrases that best describe the picture.

再會

再好不過

再跳一下

再吃一個

再見

唸唸看
Read-Aloud

- 天已經黑了。

  It's already dark.

- 弟弟想要再玩一下。

  (My) little brother wants to play a bit more.

- 媽媽說要回家了。

  Mom says (it's time to) go home.

- 弟弟只好和大家說再見。

  (My) little brother says goodbye to everyone.

- 弟弟說：「太好玩了，我以後還要再來。」

  (My) little brother says, "(That was) so much fun, I will come back again."

恭喜你完成了這一課，請回到第一頁將本課的愛心塗上顏色。

Congratulations! You have completed a lesson. Please color the heart for this lesson on page 1.

第二十五課

Lesson 25 Xiān – first; prior; in advance

本書中的國字筆順是依據中華民國教育部「常用國字標準字體筆順學習網」的筆劃順序彙編。
The stroke orders of the characters in this workbook follow the stroke orders provided on the "Learning Program for Stroke Order of Frequently Used Chinese Characters" website of the Ministry of Education, R.O.C. (Taiwan).

請將下方的字格剪下來讓孩子選擇正確的字貼上。
Please cut out the characters at the bottom and paste the correct ones.

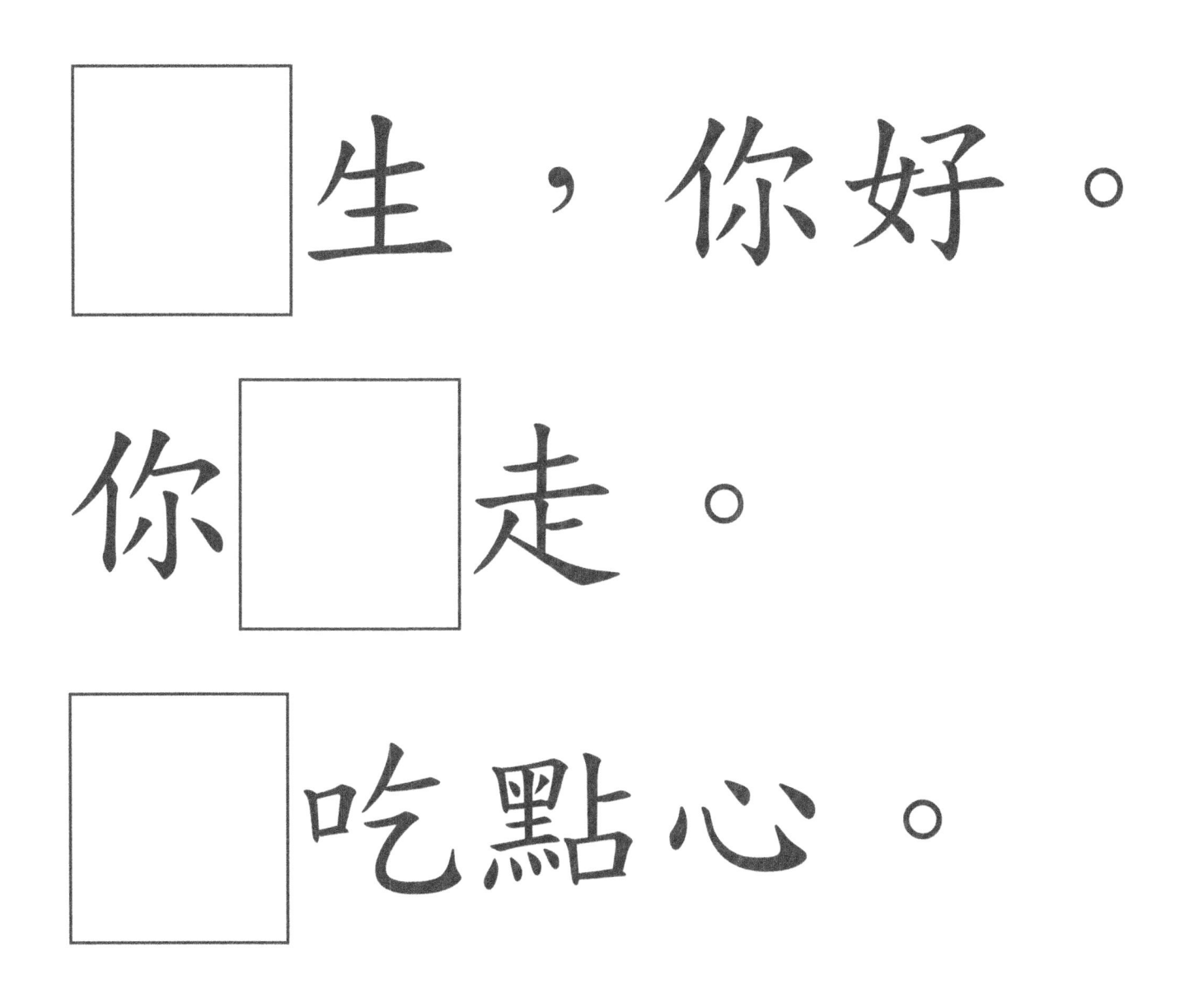

☐生，你好。

你☐走。

☐吃點心。

先　牛　先　生　先

將有「先」字的柿子著色。
Color the persimmon with the character 先.

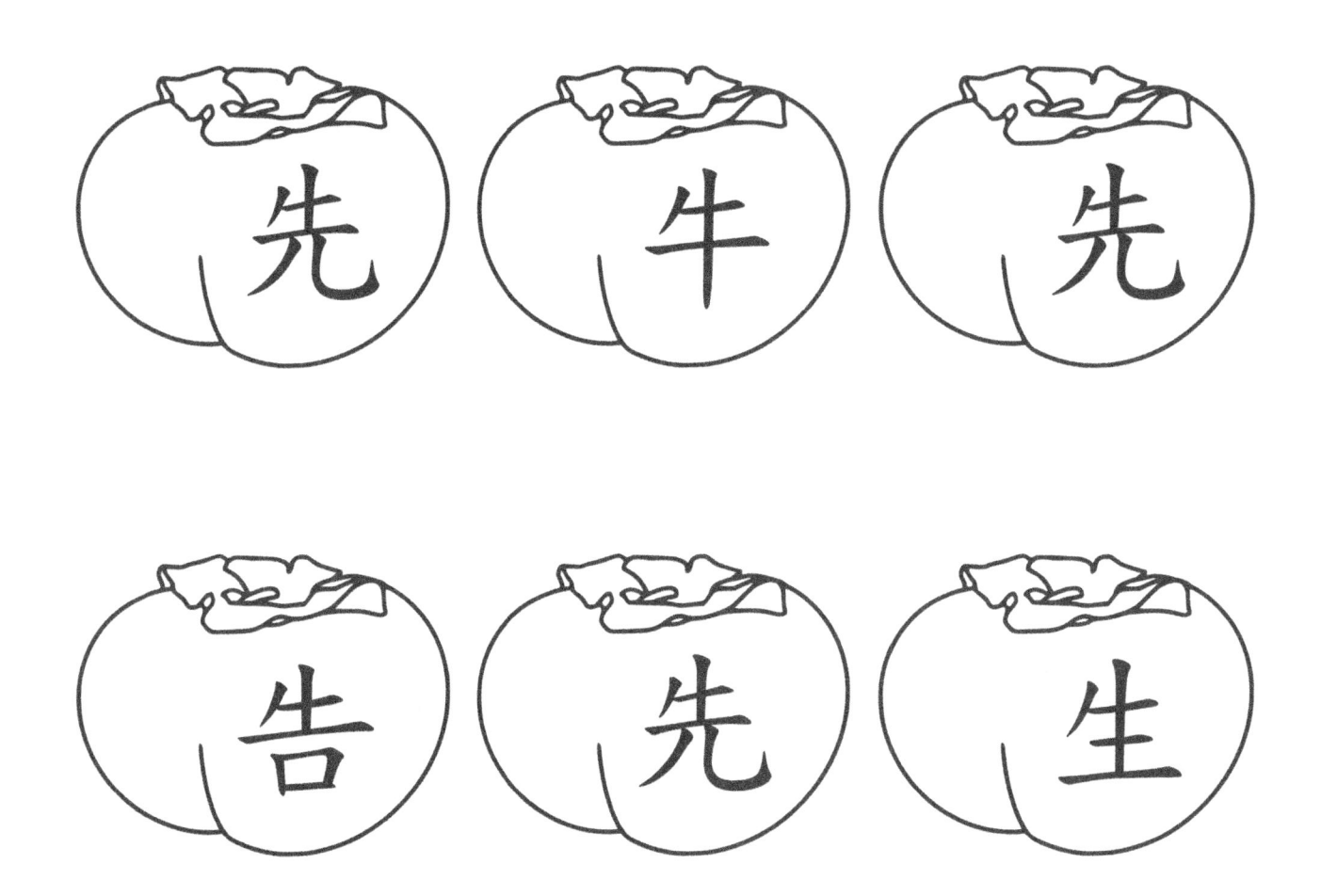

先	牛	先
告	先	生

唸唸看
Read-Aloud

- 媽媽先生我再生弟弟。
  Mom gave birth to me first and then gave birth to my little brother.

- 我先出生所以弟弟生出來時我已經很大了。
  I was born first, so when (my) little brother was born, I was already grown.

- 天黑時我會說故事給弟弟聽。
  When it's dark, I will tell (my) little brother stories.

- 弟弟長大後會和我一起玩。
  (My) little brother will play with me when (he) grows up.

恭喜你完成了這一課,請回到第一頁將本課的愛心塗上顏色。
Congratulations! You have completed a lesson. Please color the heart for this lesson on page 1.

獎狀
Certificate of Achievement

恭喜
Congratulations to

完成趣味識字第六冊。
特發此狀以資鼓勵！

for completing Fun with Chinese Workbook 6.

簽名 Signature

日期 Date